F-105
THUNDER CHIEF

in detail & scale

Bert Kinzey

KALMBACH BOOKS

Airlife Publishing Ltd.
England

CONTRIBUTORS

Ray Leader	Bill Malerba
George Cockle	Robert J. Mills
Al Lloyd	Rick Alexander
Gerald McMasters	Bill Spidle
Warren Munkasy	Cliff Bossie
Don Schmenk	Tom Copeland
Bob Johnson	Ron Thurlow
Bob Leavitt	The U.S. Air Force

Detail & Scale would like to express a special thanks to LTC George Graves, Major Bruce Maclane, and Captain Charles ''Chuck'' Buncher of the 128th Tactical Fighter Squadron (George Air National Guard) for their cooperation and assistance during the preparation of this book.

The author would like to express a special thanks to Ray Leader who took many of the photos used in this book. On numerous occasions Ray traveled to Dobbins Air Force Base to take and retake special detail photographs specifically for this book. He did excellent work, and got the exact photographs he was asked for. This resulted in a much better and more complete book than it would have been without his help. His efforts required a great deal of time and expense, and although Ray has contributed to almost all of the books in the Detail & Scale series, his work is deserving of special note here.

Most photographs in this book are credited to their contributors. Photos with no credit indicated were taken by the author.

Dedicated to:
DAVID M. ROEDER

F-105 pilot with 100 combat missions
B-52 pilot with 48 combat missions
American held hostage in Iran for 444 days
Free American
Admired Friend

FIRST EDITION
FIFTH PRINTING

Cataloging-in-Publication Data

Kinzey, Bert
    F-105 Thunderchief in detail & scale / by Bert Kinzey.
        p.   cm. -- (D&S ; vol. 8)
        Originally published: Blue Ridge Summit, PA : TAB Books. c1982.
        ISBN 0-89024-164-3 : $11.95
        1. Thunderchief (Fighter plane)   I. Title.
[UG1242.F5K537   1993]
623.74'64--dc20
                                3-20524
                                    CIP

Published in Great Britain by

Airlife Publishing Ltd.
St. Johns Hill
Shrewsbury, SY1 1JE

British Library Cataloging in Publication Data:
Kinzey, Bert
F-105 Thunderchief in detail & scale.
1. Thunderchief (Fighter Planes)
I.Title
623.74'63   TL685.3
ISBN 0-85368-554-1

Front Cover: An F-105G of the Georgia Air National Guard shows its teeth to the camera. The F-105 was always an awesome looking fighter from almost any angle.
Rear Cover: Instrument panel in the front cockpit of an F-105G.

INTRODUCTION

Head-on view of an F-105B in wrap-around camouflage.   *(Cockle)*

As this book is released and begins to appear on the bookshelves of aviation enthusiasts, the "Thud" will be disappearing from the skies over America. As this is written, only a handful of F-105s remain, and they are all scheduled for a final flight to the "boneyard" in the very near future. Hopefully, museums will preserve a number of these machines for future generations of airplane lovers to see, and others will become gate guards and display aircraft at air bases. Certainly the Thunderchief deserves appropriate preservation. Of all the "Century Series" of fighters, it saw more combat, and served this nation more admirably in war than any of the others. It was entirely an American aircraft, serving only in the colors of the United States. Of all the other "Century Series" fighters, only the F-106 Delta Dart has served only in the United States Air Force. All others have been exported to at least one foreign country.

Of the many F-105 pilots this author has known, most with combat experience, all loved this aircraft. They had admiration for its ruggedness and durability, its bomb-carrying capability, and most of all, its capability to leave the target area and "go home at the speed of light!"

The Thunderchief was designed to deliver a nuclear weapon at supersonic speed - a mission it never was called upon to perform. Instead, it deli-

vered more conventional bombs to Route Pac 6, and "Downtown Hanoi" than any other fighter. In doing so it suffered the greatest number of losses over any other aircraft, but considering the number of missions flown, the loss rate was not so high. It also was used as a "Wild Weasel" aircraft, to attack enemy air defense missile sites, a role in which it proved very adapt, and for which it received a great deal of publicity.

Detail & Scale has made every effort to provide the most detailed coverage of the F-105 that is possible. Many lengthy trips were made and many photos taken in order to make this book as complete as possible. In order to present as many of these photos as possible, we have held our usual historical summary and other write-ups to an absolute minimum. We believe it is more important to present the Thud in as great amount of detail as possible, and let our readers take a good close look. There will never be an opportunity to get these photos again.

This book marks a first for Detail & Scale in that it is the first book that we have ever dedicated to an individual. The dedication is to Colonel David Roeder who flew 100 combat missions in the F-105 in Vietnam and 48 missions in a B-52. He was a hostage in Iran for 444 days, but is now a free American. He is a true, real American, and an admired friend.

3

HISTORICAL SUMMARY

F-105D-15-RE, 61-0079, in an early bare metal scheme. The buzz numbers on the F-105 were carried on the nose under the U.S. Air Force. *(via I.A.A.P.)*

Republic's Model AP 63-31 was a private venture that was begun even before its predecessor, the F-84F Thunderstreak, entered service with the U.S. Air Force. Envisioned as a Mach 1.5 aircraft, the final design was a single-seat, single-engine, fighter-bomber capable of delivering nuclear weapons, and also having an air-to-air capability.

In April 1952, Republic submitted the proposal for the AP 63-31 to the Air Force, and it was endorsed the following month. However no general operational requirements (GOR) were issued at that time. A letter contract was issued in September 1952, and later modified to include 37 F-105s and 9 RF-105s.

The mockup inspection was in October 1953, and delivery of the first aircraft was planned for early 1955. It was to be powered by a J71 engine, but in January 1954 this was changed to the J75 engine. This was concurrent with reinstatement of the F-105 program after a two month suspension brought about by excessive delays.

In February 1955 the Air Force again changed the number of aircraft ordered to 15, to include 2 -As, 10 -Bs, and 3 RF-105s. The first of these, the initial YF-105A, first flew on October 22, 1955, and the second YF-105A flew on January 28th of the following year. These were the only two YF-105As built, and the first sustained major damage in a landing accident during the test program.

The F-105B was the first model to be accepted by the Air Force for operational service. This occurred on May 27, 1958, and the F-105 thus became the first operational aircraft designed as a fighter-bomber.

The F-105B was selected for use by the "Thunderbirds," but an accident in May 1964 caused the team to change back to F-100s until the F-105B could be modified. However the F-105 never returned to the "Thunderbirds," who flew the F-100s until they were replaced by F-4Es in 1969.

The F-105D followed the F-105B into production after the F-105C, a proposed two-seat trainer with a bubble canopy, was cancelled. The F-105D had the higher thrust J75-P-19W engine with water injection. Some tape type instruments were added in the cockpit, and attack and navigation systems were

The YF-105A prototype shows its area rule fuselage, distinctive intakes, and nose probe in this photo. Also note the pitot boom on the left wing tip. F-105Bs originally had their pitot booms located on the wing tip. Another distinctive feature of the prototype was the small windows located on either side of the spine just behind the cockpit. *(via Alexander)*

4

GENERAL ARRANGEMENT

1. AMMUNITION DRUM
2. AIR REFUELING RECEPTACLE & PROBE
3. ATM (AIR TURBINE MOTOR)
4. OPTICAL SIGHT
5. EJECTION SEAT
6. **F** ONLY REAR EJECTION SEAT
7. FORWARD FUEL TANK
8. MAIN FUEL TANK
9. LE FLAP
10. TE FLAP
11. AFT FUEL TANK
12. ENGINE
13. WATER TANK
14. POSITION LIGHTS (3)
15. RUDDER
16. DRAG CHUTE COMPT
17. SPEED BRAKES
18. STABILIZER
19. ARRESTING HOOK
20. AILERON
21. WING PYLON TANK
22. SPOILERS
23. TAXI LIGHT
24. CENTERLINE PYLON TANK

Courtesy of the U.S.A.F.

25. BOMB BAY TANK
26. AUX ELECTRONIC COMPT
27. EXTERNAL ELECTRICAL POWER RECEPTACLE
28. LEFT ELECTRONIC COMPT
29. LANDING LIGHT
30. BATTERY
31. M-61 GUN
32. LIQUID OXYGEN CONVERTER
33. FWD ELECTRONIC COMPT
34. PITOT BOOM

improved. Later, all F-105B/Ds received both the probe and drogue and the high speed boom refueling capabilities during project "Look Alike."

The most noticeable difference between the -D and earlier -B was the longer nose housing the R-12 radar. But there were other changes that were less noticeable. For example, the higher gross weight of the -D necessitated a stronger main gear and brakes.

It was the F-105D that was first sent to Vietnam, and it was followed by the F-105F and F-105G. First use of the Thunderchief in combat was in early 1965. This combat led to modifications and improvements. These included armor plating, the ASG-19 bombsight, X-band beacons, backup flight control systems, new radar altimeters, improved ejection seats, and radar homing and warning (RHAW) gear were added. Thirty F-105Ds received the Thunderstick II modification which involved increasing the size of the spine of the aircraft. Additionally, to help counter the surface-to-air missile threat, the F-105 was modified to carry ECM pods, and as such was the first U.S. fighter so equipped.

A reconnaissance version of the F-105D was proposed, but finally cancelled in favor of the forthcoming RF-4C.

The F-105F was basically a two-seat F-105D. It had a higher vertical tail with a broader chord, a longer fuselage (by 31 inches), and a 2,000 pound higher gross weight. The 143 F-105Fs produced were actually converted from the last 143 F-105Ds scheduled for production. No F-105Fs were actually procured as -Fs from the beginning.

Because of the similarity to the F-105D, the -F suffered the same problems of the F-105D, received the same solutions, and also received the improvements and modifications for the combat missions in Vietnam.

In January 1965, modifications were undertaken on 86 F-105Fs to improve their capability against the Soviet-built SAMs in Vietnam. These aircraft replaced the F-100Fs being used in this role and named "Wild Weasels." This "Wild Weasel III" modification was completed in March 1968. Subsequent modifications and improvements, which allowed the F-105 to launch the AGM-78B Standard ARM, resulted in a redesignation to F-105G for the aircraft so modified.

As the war in Vietnam continued, the losses of F-105s grew, and, for a time, consideration was given to reopening the F-105 production line. However this proposal was never realized, and, after the war, surviving aircraft were transferred to the Air Force Reserve and Air National Guard to serve out the remainder of their operational life.

VARIABLE AIR INLETS

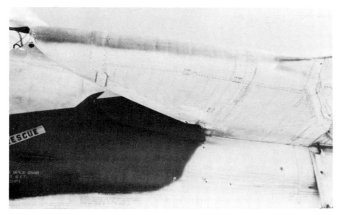

The F-105 had distinctive air inlets at the root of each wing. This photo shows the left inlet detail.

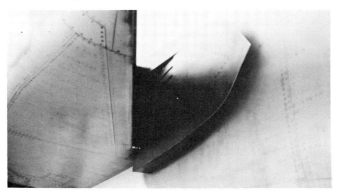

Right inlet showing the boundary layer fence located next to the fuselage.

Head-on view of the left inlet with FOD cover in place. Note the brace on the cover.

VARIABLE AIR INLETS

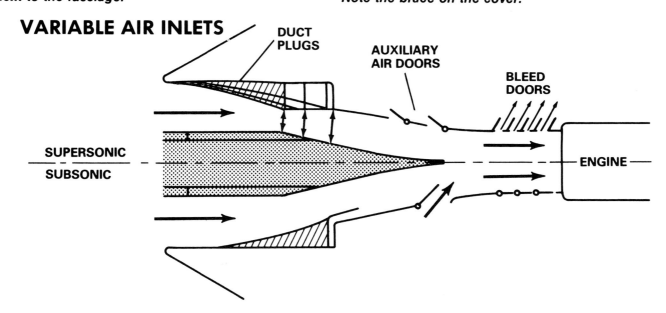

DUCT PLUGS

DUCT PLUG MOVEMENT FORWARD AND AFT AS A FUNCTION OF MACH NUMBER VARIES THE SIZE OF THE DUCT THROAT AT SPEEDS ABOVE APPROXIMATELY MACH 1.5.

Courtesy of the U.S.A.F.

AUXILIARY AIR INLETS

THE AUXILIARY AIR INLETS ARE OPENED BY DIFFERENTIAL AIR PRESSURE. WHEN NEGATIVE PRESSURE EXISTS IN THE DUCTS THE AIR INLETS OPEN PROVIDED THE LANDING GEAR IS EXTENDED. WHEN THE LANDING GEAR IS RETRACTED, A MECHANICAL INTERLOCK KEEPS THE INLETS CLOSED.

BLEED DOORS

BLEED DOORS ARE POSITIONED AS A FUNCTION OF MACH NO. AND TOTAL TEMPERATURE. EXCESS AIR, WHICH WOULD TEND TO FORCE THE SHOCK WAVE OUT OF THE DUCT THROAT, IS DUMPED.

ANTENNA LOCATIONS

F-105B ANTENNAS

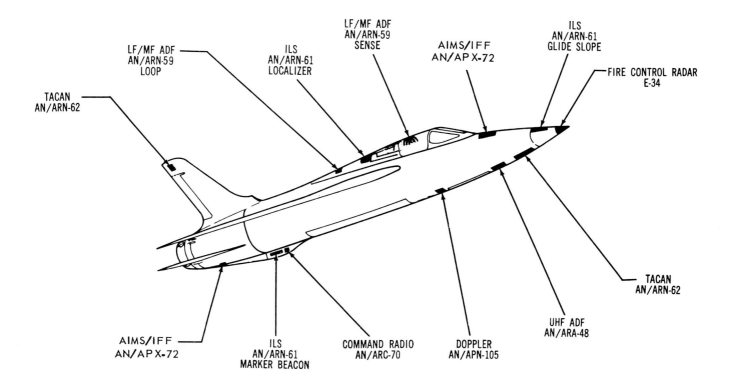

TACAN
AN/ARN-62

LF/MF ADF
AN/ARN-59
LOOP

ILS
AN/ARN-61
LOCALIZER

LF/MF ADF
AN/ARN-59
SENSE

AIMS/IFF
AN/APX-72

ILS
AN/ARN-61
GLIDE SLOPE

FIRE CONTROL RADAR
E-34

TACAN
AN/ARN-62

UHF ADF
AN/ARA-48

AIMS/IFF
AN/APX-72

ILS
AN/ARN-61
MARKER BEACON

COMMAND RADIO
AN/ARC-70

DOPPLER
AN/APN-105

F-105D & F ANTENNAS

(F-105G antennas are similar, but additional special antennas have been added.)

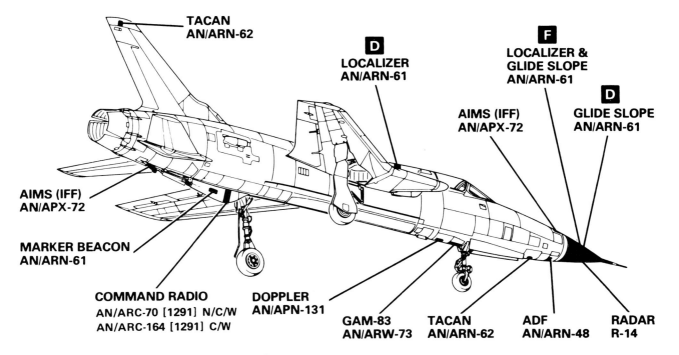

TACAN
AN/ARN-62

D LOCALIZER
AN/ARN-61

F LOCALIZER &
GLIDE SLOPE
AN/ARN-61

AIMS (IFF)
AN/APX-72

D GLIDE SLOPE
AN/ARN-61

AIMS (IFF)
AN/APX-72

MARKER BEACON
AN/ARN-61

COMMAND RADIO
AN/ARC-70 [1291] N/C/W
AN/ARC-164 [1291] C/W

DOPPLER
AN/APN-131

GAM-83
AN/ARW-73

TACAN
AN/ARN-62

ADF
AN/ARN-48

RADAR
R-14

Courtesy of the U.S.A.F.

In-flight shot of an F-105D-31-RE, 62-4353, of the 466th Tactical Fighter Squadron, 508th Tactical Fighter Group, Air Force Reserve at Hill AFB, Utah.   (Cockle)

An F-105D-15-RE of the same unit as the aircraft above. This aircraft carries a wrap-around camouflage scheme, and a travel pod on the centerline multiple ejector rack (MER).   (Cockle)

The last F-105D-20-RE built, 61-0161, flies on the wing of an F-105F-1-RE, 63-8351, during final approach for landing.   (via I.A.A.P.)

Head-on view of an F-105G Wild Weasel on the ramp at Dobbins AFB, Georgia.   (Leader)

EJECTION SEAT DETAIL

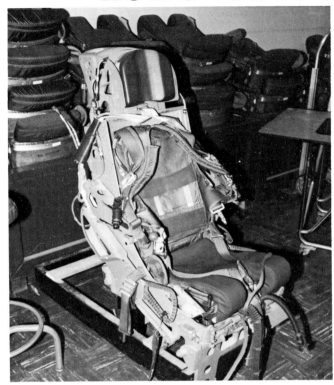

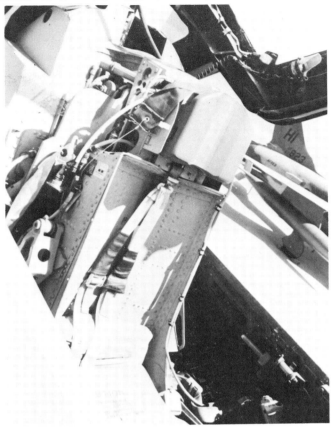

Above left: Fully equipped seat removed from the aircraft. The parachute pack is in place, but is not normally stored in the aircraft.   *(Johnson)*

Above right: Ejection seat from the right as installed in an F-105D.

Below left: Top of seat and area behind showing canopy hinge mechanism on an F-105B.

Below right: Looking down on an ejection seat as it is normally installed in the aircraft without the parachute. The survival pack is in the seat cushion.

J75 ENGINE

Engine removed from the aircraft for maintenance.

Close-up of the afterburner section on the J75 engine.

Removal of the engine from the aircraft means removing most of the rear end of the fuselage and the tail section.

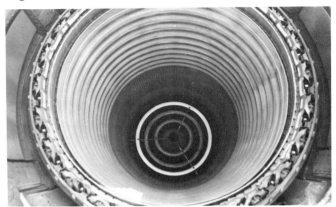

Looking up the afterburner can on an engine installed in an F-105G.

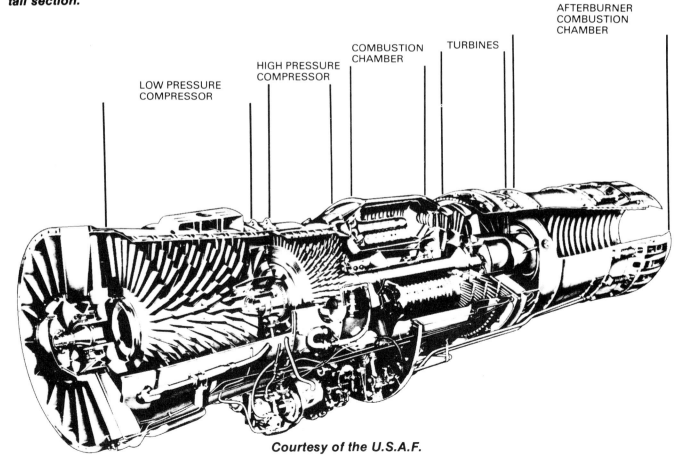

LOW PRESSURE COMPRESSOR

HIGH PRESSURE COMPRESSOR

COMBUSTION CHAMBER

TURBINES

AFTERBURNER COMBUSTION CHAMBER

Courtesy of the U.S.A.F.

10

NOSE LANDING GEAR

Nose landing gear from the front. Note the landing and taxi lights, and the covered GCA antenna directly above them.

Nose gear from the left. Note the various electrical and hydraulic lines on the strut.

Nose gear from behind and to the right. Landing gear on F-105s is usually painted aluminum, however gray is sometimes used.

Nose gear well looking aft.

LEFT MAIN LANDING GEAR

Left main landing gear from behind and to the right.

Left main gear from the front. Note the light and the hydraulic lines.

Outer portion of the left main gear well. Forward is to the bottom of the photograph. Reinforcing "band-aid" strips of metal can be seen in this photo immediately in front of and to the rear of the struts. These strengthened the wing, and added more hours of life to the aging Thunderchief.

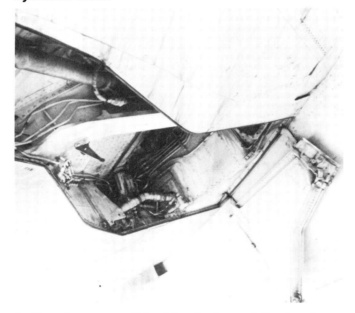

Left main gear well looking in toward the fuselage. Note the door hanging down next to the fuselage, and the numerous lines and fittings inside the well. In some cases, wheel wells are painted a dark chromate green, such as shown in the photo to the left, but in other cases, they are white or the same light gray as the underside of the aircraft as shown here.

RIGHT MAIN LANDING GEAR

Right main gear from the outside.

Right main gear detail from the inside.

Right main gear from the front. Note the angle of the doors.

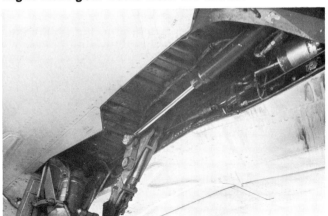

Right main gear well looking out toward the strut.

Inner portion of the right main gear well showing connectors and lines.

F-105B

F-105B-20-RE, 57-823, in the closing days of its service life.   *(Cockle)*

The YF-105B first flew on May 26, 1956, but was damaged on landing, thus resulting in a delay in the flight test program.

The first production F-105B was accepted on May 27, 1958, and entered operational service with the 335th Tactical Fighter Squadron, 4th Fighter Wing, in August 1958.

The first production blocks of F-105Bs, the F-105B-10-REs and F-105B-15-REs, were initially powered by the J75-P-5 engine, but the F-105B-20-REs were given the J75-P-19 with an additional 1000 pounds of thrust. Subsequently, this engine was retrofitted to the earlier aircraft.

Problems persisted with the F-105 for some time and none of the aircraft were operationally ready until after March 1960. The most significant problems centered around the autopilot, central air data computer, and the MA-8 fire control system. Additionally, a severe shortage of spare parts kept many aircraft out of service. These problems continued through 1961, and the F-105B was requiring 150 maintenance hours for one flying hour.

One bright spot in the early life of the F-105B was the setting of a world speed record on December 11, 1959. In establishing this record, an F-105B flew 1,216.48 mph over a 100 kilometer closed course at Edwards AFB, California.

Beginning in 1964, TAC began phasing out its two squadrons of F-105Bs, and replaced them with the F-105Ds. A total of seventy-five -Bs was accepted, thirteen of which were test and evaluation aircraft. Three TF-105Bs were used in the development of the RF-105 which was later cancelled. It is interesting to note that some of these F-105Bs soldiered on until 1981 before finally being sent to the boneyard. These -Bs served with the New Jersey Air National Guard and the 508th Tactical Fighter Group, Air Force Reserve, at Hill AFB, Utah.

Right side of the same aircraft as above showing the wrap-around camouflage to good effect.   *(Cockle)*

F-105B TECHNICAL DATA

Description

The principal mission of the F-105B is that of a fighter bomber.

This airplane is a thin mid-wing swept wing aircraft with a low position maneuvering stabilizer, spoiler-aileron combination full span leading edge flaps, and 3/4 span trailing edge flaps. The fuselage incorporates a bomb bay capable of housing either a special store or an auxiliary fuel tank.

Other features include a supersonic, variable area wing root air inlet duct, cockpit pressurization, liquid oxygen system, hydraulic power-operated irreversible flight controls with artifical "feel" large speed brakes located at the aft end of the fuselage, integrated automatic flight control system, "probe-drogue" in-flight refueling provisions, single point re-fueling, nose wheel steering, braking parachute, and a self-contained doppler navigator.

The MA-8 Fire Control System, consisting of the E-50 Sighting System in conjunction with the E-34 Radar Ranging System, and E-30 Toss Bomb Computer.

Wing Area	385 sq. ft.	Wing Section
Aspect Ratio	3.18	(root-sta. 80) .... NACA 65A-005.5
M.A.C.	137.76 in.	(tip) .... NACA 65A-003.7

POWER PLANT

Nr & Model	(1) J75-P-19
Mfr	Pratt & Whitney
Engine Spec Nr	A-2607C
Type	Two Spool Axial
Length	259.3"
Diameter	43.0"
Weight(dry)	5950 lb
Tail Pipe	Two Position Convergent with Republic Ram Air Ejector
Augmentation	Afterburning

ENGINE RATINGS

SLS	LB - RPM † - MIN
Max:	*24,500 - 6400/8990 - 5
Mil:	16,100 - 6440/9000 - 30
Nor:	14,300 - 6080/8750 - Cont

* With afterburner operating
† First figure represents RPM of the low pressure spool while the second that of the high pressure spool.

ELECTRONICS

Comm-Ident-Navig Subsystem	AN/ASQ-37
UHF Command	AN/ARC-70
Direction Finder	AN/ARA-48
Marker Beacon	AN/ARN-61
TACAN	AN/ARN-62
IFF/SIF	AN/APX-37
Intercom	AN/AIC-20
Automatic ADF	AN/ARN-59
Doppler Navigation	AN/APN-105
Fire Control System(mod)	MA-8
Autopilot(AFCS)	AF/A42G-1 (XK-5)

WEIGHTS

Loading	Lb	L. F.
Empty	25,855 (A)	
Basic	26,305	
Design	↓ 31,392	8.67 (7.33)
Combat	*34,870	
Max T.O.	‡‡ 52,000	2.00
Max Land	†† 32,167	

(A) Actual
† No store

* For Basic Mission
‡‡ Limited by structure
†† Limited by rate of sink
Note: Load factors in ( ) are for supersonic maneuvers.

FUEL

Location	Nr Tanks	Gal
Fuselage	7	†1160
Fus, bomb bay	1	390
Wgs, ext, drop	2	900
Fus, ext, drop	1	*650
	Total	†3100
*450 (optional)	Total	†2900

† Includes 25 gal in tank lines
Grade JP-4
Specification MIL-J-5624

OIL

Engine, integral . 1 ... (tot) 4.5
Specification MIL-L-7808

GUNS

Nr	Type	Size	Rds ea	Loc
1	M-61	20mm	1075	Fus

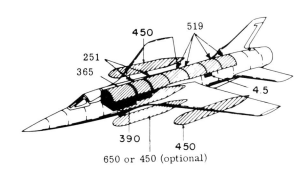

NOTE: Total internal fuel equals 1160 gal of which 25 gal of useable fuel is located in the fuel lines.

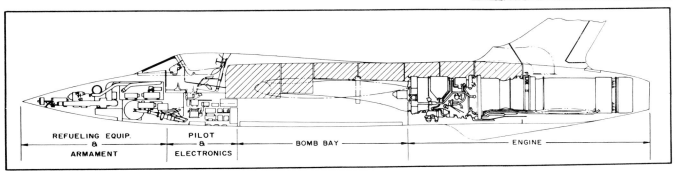

Courtesy of the U.S.A.F.

F-105B PERFORMANCE DATA

Loading and Performance—Typical Mission

CONDITIONS			BASIC MISSION I	DESIGN MISSION II	DESIGN MISSION III	GROUND SUPPORT IV	FERRY RANGE V
TAKE-OFF WEIGHT	(lb)		46,998	46,998	49,566	48,822	46,979
Fuel at 6.5 lb/gal (grade JP-4)	(lb)		16,315	16,315	18,850	18,850	18,850
Payload (Ammo)	(lb)		724	724	724	712 ⑥	724
Payload (Bombs)	(lb)	⑤	---	---	1598	---	None
Wing loading	(lb/sq ft)		122.1	122.1	128.7	126.8	122.0
Stall speed (power off)	(kn)		177	177	182	180	177
Take-off ground run at SL	(ft)	①	4450	4450	5020	4850	4450
Take-off to clear 50 ft	(ft)	①	6220	6220	7100	6830	6220
Rate of climb at SL	(fpm)	②	5710	5710	4405	4800	5715
Time: SL to 20,000 ft	(min)	②	4.0	4.0	5.47	5.06	4.0
Time: SL to 30,000 ft	(min)	② ⑪	7.8	7.3	13.41	11.69	7.8
Service ceiling (100 fpm)	(ft)	②	32,750	32,750	28,200	29,400	32,750
COMBAT RANGE	(n mi)		---	---	---	---	1935
COMBAT RADIUS	(n mi)	⑩	566(646)	690	767	581	---
Average cruise speed	(kn)		508	507	499	502	506
Initial cruising altitude	(ft)		25,500	29,500	26,750	27,500	29,550
Final cruising altitude	(ft)		39,000	39,400	39,400	38,800	40,600
Total mission time	(hr)		2.3	2.68	3.05	2.63	3.81
COMBAT WEIGHT	(lb)	① ⑨	34,870	33,925(35,885)	34,590(36,453)	36,834	28,819
Combat altitude	(ft)	①	S.L.	S.L.(35,400)	S.L.(35,500)	S.L.	40,600
Combat speed	(kn)	① ⑧	750	750(820)	750(741)	750	1168
Combat climb	(fpm)	①	33,800	34,800(7750)	34,100(7500)	32,000	8050
Combat ceiling (500 fpm)	(ft)	①	48,100	48,600(47,500)	48,250(45,900)	47,100	51,500
Service ceiling (100 fpm)	(ft)	②	40,700	41,250(40,200)	40,850(37,950)	39,700	44,750
Max rate of climb at SL	(fpm)	②	33,800	34,800(32,900)	34,100(27,780)	32,000	41,100
Max speed at 36,089 ft	(kn)	①	1195	1197(1194)	1196(995)	1193	1204
Basic speed at S,L,	(kn/ft)		750	750	750	750	750
LANDING WEIGHT	(lb)		29,250	28,633	28,763	29,576	28,819
Ground roll at SL	(ft)		4460	4390	4400	4500	4410
Ground roll (auxiliary brake)	(ft)	⑦	2370	2330	2340	2400	2350
Total time 50 ft	(ft)		6180	6080	6100	6240	6110
Total from 50 ft (auxiliary brake)	(ft)	⑦	4100	4020	4030	4130	4040

NOTES

① Maximum power
② Military power
③ DELETED
④ One MK28 store-internal
⑤ 2 x 750 lb bombs-external
⑥ 38 x FFA Rockets and expendable launcher cones
⑦ With 20 ft dia braking parachute
⑧ Speed at end of 3 minute run-in to target, after-burner
⑨ Values in parentheses indicate performance with store (or bombs & pylons, or rockets & launchers) aboard
⑩ Wing tanks with 1278 lb of fuel are dropped prior to combat. Radius in parentheses is calculated carrying wing tanks into combat. F-105 Type II tanks are stressed compatible with external bombs which are carried in combat
⑪ Centerline tank & pylons dropped during initial climb (27,900 ft for Basic Mission)

Courtesy of the U.S.A.F.

F-105B COCKPIT

F-105B main instrument panel. Note that the F-105B used round instruments exclusively rather than some of the tape type instruments used on later versions.

Top of instrument panel and gun sight glass in an F-105B.

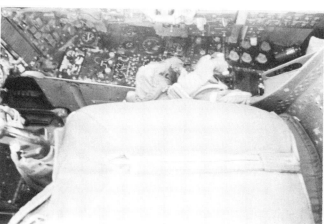

Right console and sidewall detail.

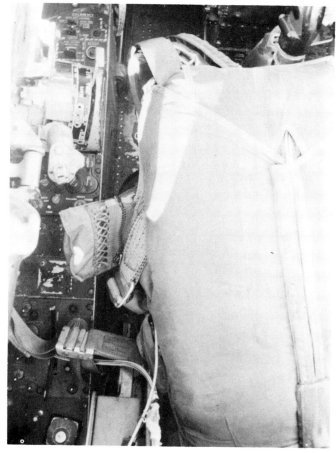

Left console and throttle from above.

Pilot in an F-105B cockpit poised for take-off. Note the antennas in the canopy glass. This was a distinctive feature of the F-105B.

F-105B WALK-AROUND

The cannon muzzle opening is much further forward on the F-105B than on later versions. This is because the -B did not have the R-14 radar, and therefore had a shorter nose.

Open panel showing the gun breech and ammunition feed mechanism. The cannon on the F-105B was more difficult to get to and service than on later versions.

Open probe and drogue type refueling probe on the left side of the nose of an F-105B. Also note the new location of the pitot probe. Another probe is on the right side.

Close-up of the open canopy showing the large hinge arrangement. Note the LF/MF ADF AN/ARN-59 SENSE antenna in the canopy glass.

Open access panel door located just ahead of the bomb bay on the left side. The crew chief checks circuit breakers inside the aircraft through this door just prior to take-off.

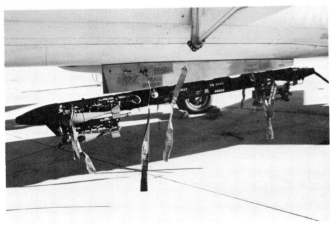

Multiple ejector rack loaded with small practice bombs. These bombs resemble bazooka rockets or mortar rounds, but have the same ballistic characteristics as the real thing.

Left wing tip detail on an F-105B. Originally, the pitot probe was located here, but it was later moved to the sides of the nose.

Left rear fuselage section showing the afterburner cooling scoop that was added to all F-105s. Also visible are the arresting hook and saber drain.

Right side of nose showing the pitot probe and angle of attack (AOA) vane. The three small gauges just ahead of the pitot probe are for the hydraulic accumulators.

Engine exhaust nozzle detail. The shell around the engine consists of four speed brakes. The lower brake usually hangs down to some degree when the aircraft is on the ground.

Underside of nose showing a position light and the TACAN and UHF ADF antennas. The E-34 fire control antenna is housed inside the small radome.

F-105D

An F-105D-31-RE, 62-4353, shows the changes over the F-105B, most noticeably the longer nose and bigger radome. *(Cockle)*

The F-105D was the most widely produced Thunderchief variant with a total of 610 being accepted. It was a considerable improvement over the F-105B, and had a J75-P-19W engine with water injection. The first flight was made on June 9, 1959, and the first -D was accepted by the Air Force on September 28, 1960 at Nellis AFB. It entered operational service with the 4th Tactical Fighter Wing in early 1961, and was delivered to USAFE's 36th TFW in May 1961. PACAF did not receive any -Ds until October 1962.

The real story of the F-105D was in Vietnam where it was deployed in 1965. In Vietnam the Thud flew more strikes against the north than any other allied aircraft, and, as a result, suffered more losses. In discussing the attributes of the F-105 with a number of pilots with combat experience, all thought the Thunderchief was an excellent aircraft. The late Col. Doug Brenner, a former "Thunderbird" pilot, referred to the F-105 as the "Cadillac" of fighters. Others who flew both the F-105 and F-4 all preferred the Thunderchief for going "down town." One pilot, with a certain degree of prejudice, stated that no two-seat, two-engine aircraft could ever replace a single-seat, single-engine fighter. But the one thing they all praised was the Thud's great speed leaving the target area. Neither the MiG-17 or MiG-21 could begin to keep up with the "Lead Sled" on the deck, but one pilot claimed that the MiG-19 could do a good job of it. Other pilots claimed it was a crime that the production lines were not reopened so that war losses could be replaced.

By 1972, war losses, accidents, and normal attrition had reduced the number of -Ds to only one-quarter of the 610 produced. These were sent to the Reserve and Air National Guard leaving only F-105G "Wild Weasels" in the active inventory.

F-105D-10-RE, 60-458, from the 457th TFS, has the enlarged spine denoting the addition of the Thunderstick II modification. *(Cockle)*

F-105D TECHNICAL DATA

Courtesy of the U.S.A.F.

Description

The principal mission of the F-105D is that of an all weather fighter-bomber. R-14A Search and Ranging Radar used in conjunction with the AN/APN-131 Doppler Navigator permit navigation and weapons delivery on any target regardless of route or target weather. The radar installation also incorporates a terrain guidance mode which permits the pilot to let down through weather in unfamiliar territory and to ground "hug" to avoid detection.

This airplane is a thin mid-wing aircraft which incorporates a bomb bay capable of housing a special store or an auxiliary fuel tank. The wings are swept back and incorporate a spoiler/aileron combination for maneuvering at supersonic speeds as well as full span leading edge flaps. Trailing edge flaps are 3/4 span.

The -31 block of aircraft have the added capability of air refueling from any type of tanker. The installation of a flush mounted retractable door type air refueling receptacle provides the dual capability of utilizing either the flying boom or hose-drogue type tanker. Pilot safety is increased with the addition of a Standby Attitude Indicator, a remote UHF Indicator, and a speed brake/ engine nozzle safety interlock. Reliability and ground maintenance is improved with the addition of independent Landing Gear Uplock Indicators, elimination of speed brake sliding shields and take-off position components and improved ground cooling of the ATM. The F-105D-31RE retains all the conventional features of the previous F-105D and F-105B Blocks such as single point refueling, M-61 Vulcan Gun, large conventional and nuclear store capacity and delivery methods, braking parachute and arrestor hook.

Development

The F-105D is a development of the earlier F-105B to which has been added the higher thrust J75-P-19W engine which incorporates water injection for increased thrust at take-off and the adverse weather navigation and attack capabilities.

First flight . . . . Jun 59
First acceptance . . . . Jul 59
Production and delivery completed . . . . Feb 64

POWER PLANT

Nr & Model . . .	(1) J75-P-19W
Mfr	Pratt & Whitney
Engine Spec Nr	A-2337-A
Type	Two Spool Axial
Length	259.3"
Diameter	43.0"
Weight (dry)	5950 lb
Augmentation	Water & Afterburner
Tail Pipe .	2-Position Convergent plus Republic Ram Air Ejector

ENGINE RATINGS

SLS	LB	-	RPM	-	MIN
T.O.	*26,500-		6900/9090	-	2.5‡
Max	+24,500-		6400/8990	-	15
Mil	16,100 -		6440/9000	-	30
Nor	14,300 -		6080/8750	-	Cont

*With water and afterburner
+With afterburner operating
‡Limited by water supply

ELECTRONICS

Comm-Ident-Navig	AN/ASQ-37
UHF Command	AN/ARC-70
Director Finder	AN/ARA-48
Marker Beacon	AN/ARN-61
TACAN	AN/ARN-62
IFF/SIF	AN/APX-37
Intercom	AN/AIC-20
Doppler Navigation . .	AN/APN-131
Fire Control System . .	AN/ASG-19
RHAWS	AN/APR-25(U)-26(V)
Radar System	R-14

WEIGHTS

Loading	Lb	L.F.
Empty. . . .	26,855(A)	
Basic . . .	27,233(A)	
Design . . .	+34,058	8.67(7.33)
Combat . .	*35,637	
Max T.O. .	‡52,838	
Max Land .	++51,038	

(A) Actual
+ No store
* For Basic Mission
‡ Limited by space
++ Limited by rate of sink of 3 fps
Note: Load factors in ( ) are for supersonic maneuvers.

FUEL

Location	Nr Tanks	Gal
Fuselage	7 . . .	+1160
Fus, bomb bay . .	1 . . .	390
Wgs, ext, drop . .	2 . . .	900
Fus, ext, drop . .	1 . . .	*650
	Total	+3100

*450 (optional) . . Total +2900
+ Includes 25 gal in tank lines
Grade JP-4
Specification MIL-J-5624

OIL
Engine, integral . . 1. . (tot) 4.5
Specification MIL-L-7808

WATER
Fus, aft . . . . 1 . . (tot) 36

GUNS

Nr	Type	Size	Rds ea	Location
1	M-61	20 mm	1028	Fuselage

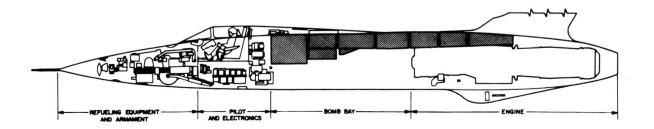

REFUELING EQUIPMENT AND ARMAMENT — PILOT AND ELECTRONICS — BOMB BAY — ENGINE

SERVICING DOORS AND PANELS

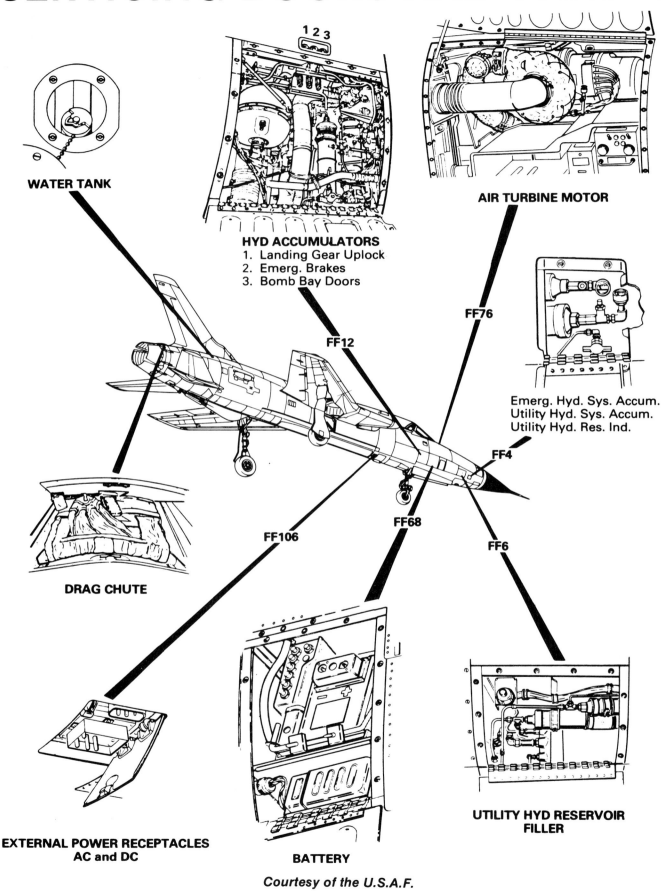

WATER TANK

HYD ACCUMULATORS
1. Landing Gear Uplock
2. Emerg. Brakes
3. Bomb Bay Doors

AIR TURBINE MOTOR

FF12

FF76

Emerg. Hyd. Sys. Accum.
Utility Hyd. Sys. Accum.
Utility Hyd. Res. Ind.

FF4

DRAG CHUTE

FF106

FF68

FF6

**EXTERNAL POWER RECEPTACLES
AC and DC**

BATTERY

**UTILITY HYD RESERVOIR
FILLER**

Courtesy of the U.S.A.F.

Water tank filler opening on the right rear fuselage.

Hydraulic accumulators located under panel FF-12.

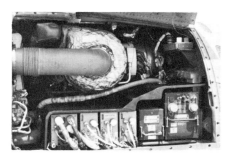

Air turbine motor.

All photos on this page are by Ray Leader.

Drag chute compartment with the chute removed.

Open panel FF4 containing the emergency hydraulic system accumulator, utility hydraulic system accumulator, and the utility hydraulic reservoir indicator.

External power receptacles.

Battery location under FF68.

Utility hydraulic reservoir filler.

Hydraulic reservoir primary, located in the left wheel well.

Engine oil gage.

Engine oil gage shutoff.

Liquid oxygen access.

Cartridge starter panel.

Arresting hook detail.

All photos on this page are by Ray Leader.

Antiskid accumulator in the nose gear well.

Single point ground refuel receptacle.

Engine oil filler location.

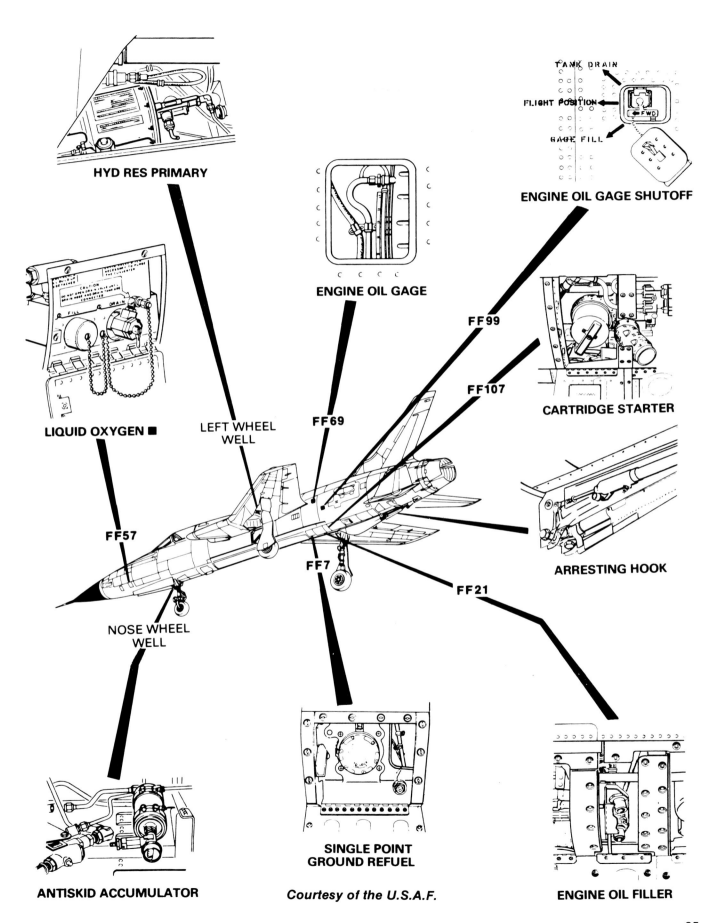

HYD RES PRIMARY

ENGINE OIL GAGE

TANK DRAIN

FLIGHT POSITION

◄ FWD

GAGE FILL

ENGINE OIL GAGE SHUTOFF

LIQUID OXYGEN ■

LEFT WHEEL WELL

FF99

FF107

CARTRIDGE STARTER

FF69

FF57

FF7

ARRESTING HOOK

FF21

NOSE WHEEL WELL

ANTISKID ACCUMULATOR

SINGLE POINT GROUND REFUEL

Courtesy of the U.S.A.F.

ENGINE OIL FILLER

F-105D PERFORMANCE DATA

Loading and Performance—Typical Mission

CONDITIONS		BASIC MISSION I (S)	HI-LO-HI II	GROUND SUPPORT III (S)	GROUND SUPPORT IV	GROUND SUPPORT V	HI-LO-LO-HI VI	FERRY RANGE VII (S)
TAKE-OFF WEIGHT	(lb)	48,976	48,976	50,231	52,093	52,813	48,840	49,371
Fuel at 6.5 lb/gal(grade JP-4)	(lb)	17,615	17,615	15,925	15,925	10,075	17,225	20,150
Payload (Ammo)	(lb)	581	581	581	581	581	581	None
Payload (Bombs)	(lb)	MK-28	MK-28	4794	6392	12,784	MK-28	None
Wing loading	(lb/sq ft)	127.2	127.2	130.5	135.3	137.2	126.9	128.2
Stall speed (power off)	(kn)	180.6	180.6	182.9	186.3	187.6	180.4	181.4
Take-off ground run at SL	(ft)	4270	4270	4520	4920	5080	4250	4350
Take-off to clear 50 ft	(ft)	5830	5830	6220	6800	7050	5800	5950
Rate of climb at SL	(fpm)	4650	4650	3900	3200	2620	4660	4600
Time: SL to 20,000 ft	(min)	5.9	5.9	7.8	9.5	12.4	5.9	6.0
Time: SL to 30,000 ft	(min)	10.15	10.15	17.0	14.6	17.1	10.3	10.4
Service ceiling (100 fpm)	(ft)	32,100	32,100	28,300	24,200	20,800	32,500	32,000
COMBAT RANGE	(n mi)	---	---	---	---	---	---	1917
COMBAT RADIUS	(n mi)	543(676)	776	506	622	277	653	---
Average cruise speed	(kn)	507	507	501	490	463	506	507
Initial cruising altitude	(ft)	30,000	30,000	26,600	22,800	18,600	30,000	29,800
Final cruising altitude	(ft)	39,450	39,600	39,200	39,500	39,500	39,500	39,400
Total mission time	(hr)	2.23	3.11	2.11	2.62	1.25	2.60	3.78
COMBAT WEIGHT	(lb)	35,637	35,402	35,568	33,841	31,554	35,397	30,172
Combat altitude	(ft)	S.L.	S.L.	S.L.	S.L.	S.L.	S.L.	39,400
Combat speed	(kn)	726	726	726	726	726	726	1182
Combat climb	(fpm)	34,000	34,200	34,000	35,800	38,500	34,200	8700
Combat ceiling (500 fpm)	(ft)	48,500	48,700	48,600	49,600	51,800	48,700	51,800
Service ceiling (100 fpm)	(ft)	41,200	41,300	41,200	42,200	43,500	41,300	44,200
Max rate of climb at SL	(fpm)	34,000	34,200	34,000	35,800	38,500	34,200	40,400
Max speed at 36,089 ft	(kn)	1192	1192	1192	1192	1198	1192	1199
Basic speed at S.L.	(kn)	726	726	726	726	726	726	726
LANDING WEIGHT	(lb)	30,118	29,437	30,284	29,577	29,577	29,595	30,172
Ground roll at SL	(ft)	4355	4270	4380	4295	4295	4295	4370
Ground roll (auxiliary brake)	(ft)	2375	2325	2390	2340	2340	2340	2380
Total from 50 ft	(ft)	6055	5940	6080	5970	5970	5970	6060
Total from 50 ft (auxiliary brake)	(ft)	4060	3990	4080	4000	4000	4000	4070

(S) MIL-C-5011A Mission

NOTES

1. Take-Off Thrust With Water Injection
2. Maximum Thrust
3. Military Thrust
4. DELETED
5. MK-28 Internal Store
6. Six M117, 750 Lb. Bombs on C/L MER
7. Six M117, 750 Lb. Bombs on C/L MER Plus Two M117, 750 Lb. Bombs Outb'd
8. Sixteen M117, 750 Lb. Bombs
9. MK-28 External Store
10. Wing Tanks with 2235 Lb. of Fuel are dropped Prior to Combat. Radius in ( ) is calculated carrying tanks in combat. F-105 Type II tanks are structurally compatible with external bombs which are carried in combat.
11. Time to Climb to 25,000 Ft. from S.L.
12. Time to Climb to 23,000 Ft. from S.L.
13. With 20 Ft. Diameter Parachute

BOMB BAY AND TANK

The F-105 had an internal bomb bay, and was designed to carry nuclear bombs. However, a bomb bay fuel tank was often carried to extend the range. The tank carried 390 gallons of fuel. Shown here are left and right side views of the bomb bay tank removed from an F-105G.

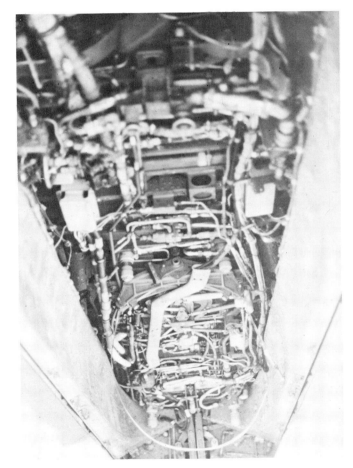 

Bomb bay looking aft.   *(Leader)*   *Close-up of the center section of the bomb bay looking forward. Note the "bomb kicker" near the center of the photo.*   *(Leader)*

PYLONS

Outboard pylon used for carrying bombs, pods, and Sidewinder launch rails. **(Thurlow)**

Outboard pylon as used for the Shrike anti-radiation missile. Compare the size and shape to the outboard pylon above. **(Levitt)**

Inboard pylon used for weapons, and, in this case, a travel pod.

Centerline pylon with fuel tank attached.

Underside view of the same pylon at top left with a base piece attached so as to allow shoulder mounting of Sidewinder missiles. **(Thurlow)**

Inboard pylon used with fuel tanks. Compare this to the pylon at left, noting that this pylon has a vertical rather than a tapered trailing edge.

Centerline pylon with MER and cluster bombs.

EXTERNAL STORE LOADING

Courtesy of the U.S.A.F.

MAXIMUM
STORE CAPABILITIES

VIEW
LOOKING
FORWARD

STORE	LEFT OUTBD	LEFT INBD	BOMB BAY	CENTER	RIGHT INBD	RIGHT OUTBD	TOTAL
SPECIAL WEAPONS							
MK-61	–	1	–	1	1	–	3
MK-57	–	–	–	1	–	–	1
CONVENTIONAL BOMBS							
MK 82 L. D.	1	4	–	6	4	1	16
MK 82 SNAKEYE M. D.	1	4	–	6	4	1	16
MK 83	1	2	–	3	2	1	9
MK 84	–	1	–	1	1	–	3
M-117 RETARDED	1	–	–	3	–	1	5
M-117 DESTRUCTOR	1	–	–	3	–	1	5
FIRE BOMBS							
BLU-27 (Finned & Unfinned)	1	2	–	2	2	1	8
CHEMICAL BOMBS							
BLU-52	1	2	–	2	2	1	8
A/B 45Y-2 (Spray Tank)	1	–	–	–	–	1	2
BOMB DISPENSERS							
SUU-10 (CBU-3)	1	–	–	–	–	1	2
SUU-30 (CBU 24, 29, 49, 53, 54)	1	4	–	5	4	1	15
SUU-13 (CBU-3, 7, 28, 37)	1	–	–	–	–	1	2
SUU-21 (Training)	1	1	–	1	1	1	5

STORE	LEFT OUTBD	LEFT INBD	BOMB BAY	CENTER	RIGHT INBD	RIGHT OUTBD	TOTAL
CONVENTIONAL BOMBS							
M-117 750 LB	1	4	-	6	4	1	16
M-118 3000 LB	-	1	-	1	1	-	3
SPECIAL WEAPONS							
MK-28 (EX and RE)	-	1	1	1	1	-	4
MK-43	-	1	1	1	1	-	4
FIRE BOMBS							
M-116A-2	1	2	-	3	2	1	9
BLU-1/B	1	2	-	3	2	1	9
CHEMICAL BOMBS							
MC-1	1	4	-	6	4	1	16
LEAFLET BOMBS							
M-129	1	4	-	6	4	1	16
BOMB DISPENSERS							
SUU-7 (CBU-1, 2, 46)	1	-	-	-	-	1	2
MN-1A (Practice Bombs)	-	1	1	1	1	-	4
MISSILES							
AIM-9B, AIM-9E	2	-	-	-	-	2	4
AGM-12C (Bullpup)	-	1	-	-	1	-	2
AGM-45A	1	-	-	-	-	1	2
ROCKET LAUNCHERS							
LAU-3/A (19 x 2.75'' Rockets)	1	2	-	-	2	1	6
LAU-18/A (19 x 2.75'' Rockets)	1	2	-	-	2	1	6
FUEL TANKS							
390 GAL	-	-	1	-	-	-	1
650 GAL	-	-	-	1	-	-	1
450 GAL	-	1	-	1	1	-	3

STORE	LEFT OUTBD	LEFT INBD	BOMB BAY	CENTER	RIGHT INBD	RIGHT OUTBD	TOTAL
MINES							
BLU-31	1	2	–	3	2	1	9
ROCKET LAUNCHERS							
LAU 32 (7 x 2.75'' Rockets)	1	2	–	–	2	1	6
LAU 59 (7 x 2.75'' Rockets)	1	2	–	–	2	1	6
FLARES							
MLU-32/B-99	–	–	–	6	–	–	6
MISC							
AN-ALE 2 (Chaff Dispenser)	1	–	–	–	–	1	2
QRC 160-1, -2, -8 (ECM POD)	1	–	–	–	–	1	2
QRC-335 (ECM POD)	1	–	–	–	–	1	2

F-105D & F COCKPIT LAYOUTS

MAIN INSTRUMENT PANEL D & F *front* F *rear*

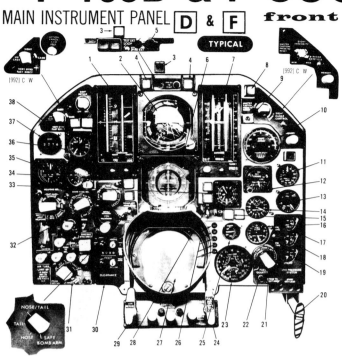

1. AMI (Airspeed Mach Indicator)
2. ADI (Attitude Director Indicator)
3. Stabilizer Lock Light [1045] C/W
4. Engine Overheat and Fire Warning Lights
5. Fire Extinguisher Button 1060 C/W
6. HSI (Horizontal Situation Indicator)
7. AVVI (Altitude-Vertical Velocity Indicator)
8. Bail-Out Light (F only)
9. Master Caution Light
10. Ground Speed and Drift Angle Indicator
11. Tachometer
12. Pressure Ratio Gage
13. Oil Pressure Gage

14. Exhaust Gas Temperature Gage
15. Fuel Leak Caution Light [1061] C/W (deactivated)
16. Fuel Flow Indicator
17. Hydraulic Pressure Gage (PRI One)
18. Hydraulic Pressure Gage (PRI Two)
19. Hydraulic Pressure Gage (Utility)
20. Emergency Brake Handle
21. Fuel Quantity Selector Switch
22. Fuel Quantity Test Button
23. Fuel Quantity Indicator
24. Auxiliary Special Weapon Release Handle
25. Antenna Tilt Indicator
26. Radar Mode Indicator Lights

27. Radar Scope
28. Steering Bar (Needle) Switch
29. Air Refuel Handle
30. Clearance Plane Indicator
31. Armament Control Panel
32. Instrument Selector Switch
33. Clock
34. Standby Attitude Indicator
35. Standby Airspeed Indicator
36. Standby Altimeter
37. Remote Channel Indicator
38. Vertical Gyro Fast Erection Button

LEFT CONSOLE TYPICAL   ## LEFT CONSOLE TYPICAL

D & F   F *rear*

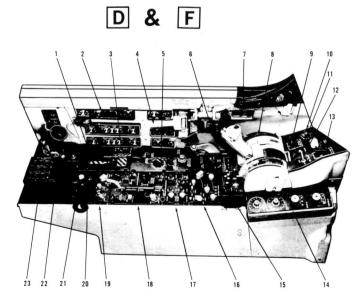

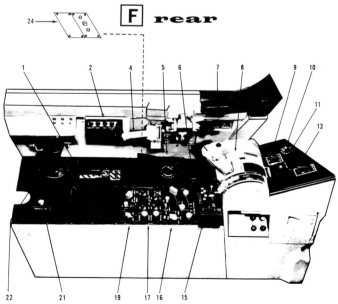

1. Auxiliary Canopy Jettison Handle
2. Circuit Breaker Panel
3. Alternate Engine Fuel Feed Switch [1061] C/W
4. Canopy Lock Lever
5. Fuel System Control Panel
6. Flight Control Panel
7. Interior Canopy Control Switch
8. Throttle Quadrant
9. Emergency Fuel System Switch
10. Flap Position Indicator
11. Air Start Button
12. Water Injection Switch

13. Bail-Out Light Switch (F Only)
14. Toss Bomb Computer Controls
15. Radar, R-14, Control Panel
16. Command Radio, AN/ARC-70, Control Panel
17. AFCS Control Panel
18. Temperature Control Panel
19. Interphone, An/AIC-20, Control Panel
20. Cockpit Utility Light F

21. Anti-G Suit Valve Test Button
22. Pilot's Relief Container
23. Special Weapons Circuit Breaker Panel
24. F Missile Audio Control [F-559] C/W

Courtesy of the U.S.A.F.

AUXILIARY INSTRUMENT PANELS **D & F**   **F** rear
TYPICAL

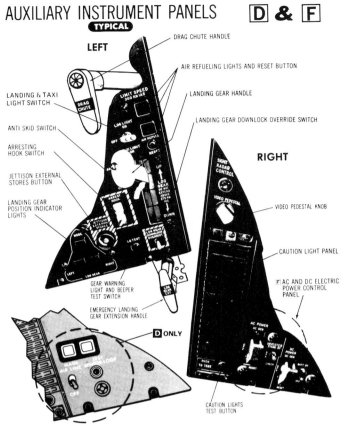

LEFT

- DRAG CHUTE HANDLE
- AIR REFUELING LIGHTS AND RESET BUTTON
- LANDING & TAXI LIGHT SWITCH
- LANDING GEAR HANDLE
- ANTI SKID SWITCH
- LANDING GEAR DOWNLOCK OVERRIDE SWITCH
- ARRESTING HOOK SWITCH
- JETTISON EXTERNAL STORES BUTTON
- **RIGHT**
- SIGHT RADAR CONTROL
- LANDING GEAR POSITION INDICATOR LIGHTS
- VIDEO PEDESTAL
- VIDEO PEDESTAL KNOB
- GEAR WARNING LIGHT AND BEEPER TEST SWITCH
- CAUTION LIGHT PANEL
- [F] AC AND DC ELECTRIC POWER CONTROL PANEL
- EMERGENCY LANDING GEAR EXTENSION HANDLE
- **D ONLY**
- CAUTION LIGHTS TEST BUTTON

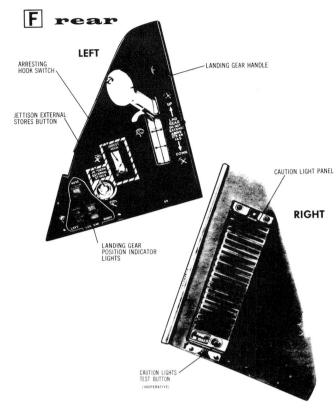

F rear

LEFT

- ARRESTING HOOK SWITCH
- LANDING GEAR HANDLE
- JETTISON EXTERNAL STORES BUTTON
- CAUTION LIGHT PANEL
- **RIGHT**
- LANDING GEAR POSITION INDICATOR LIGHTS
- CAUTION LIGHTS TEST BUTTON
- (INOPERATIVE)

Courtesy of the U.S.A.F.

RIGHT console   TYPICAL **D**

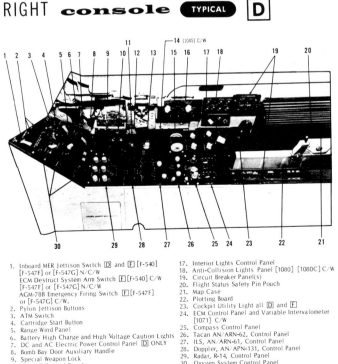

RIGHT console   TYPICAL   **F** front
TYPICAL

F rear

1. Inboard MER Jettison Switch **D** and **F** [F-540] [F-547F] or [F-547G] N/C/W
   ECM Destruct System Arm Switch **F** [F-540] C/W [F-547F] or [F-547G] N/C/W
   AGM-78B Emergency Firing Switch **F** [F-547F] or [F-547G] C/W.
2. Pylon Jettison Buttons
3. ATM Switch
4. Cartridge Start Button
5. Range Wind Panel
6. Battery High Charge and High Voltage Caution Lights
7. DC and AC Electric Power Control Panel **D** ONLY
8. Bomb Bay Door Auxiliary Handle
9. Special Weapon Lock
10. IFF/SIF Control Panels
11. Displacing Gear Pressure Indicator
12. CVDA Knob
13. CADC Self Test Switch
14. Emergency Pitch and Roll Control Switches [1045] C/W
15. Timer Control
16. Exterior Lights Control Panel
17. Interior Lights Control Panel
18. Anti-Collision Lights Panel [1080] [1080C] C/W
19. Circuit Breaker Panel(s)
20. Flight Status Safety Pin Pouch
21. Map Case
22. Plotting Board
23. Cockpit Utility Light all **D** and **F**
24. ECM Control Panel and Variable Intervalometer [1071] C/W
25. Compass Control Panel
26. Tacan AN/ARN-62, Control Panel
27. ILS, AN/ARN-61, Control Panel
28. Doppler, AN/APN-131, Control Panel
29. Radar, R-14, Control Panel
30. Oxygen System Control Panel
31. Control Transfer Panels (**F** ONLY)
32. **F** Test Airline Overheat Sensor Button
33. Aft Radar Scope Deactivate Switch (**F** Only)
34. Flight Instrument Simulate Failure Switch (**F** Only)
35. Main Airline Shutoff Valve Switch
36. ECM Destruct System Arm Switch **F** [F-547F] or [F-547G] C/W

SPECIAL WEAPONS
controls

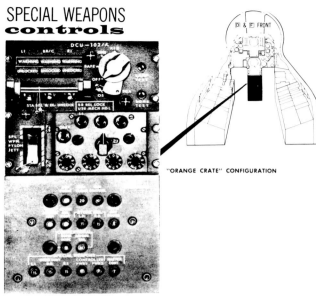

"ORANGE CRATE" CONFIGURATION

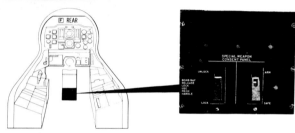

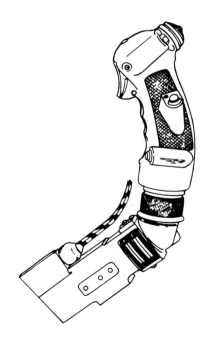

CONTROL GRIP

Courtesy of the U.S.A.F.

THROTTLE QUADRANT
D & F FRONT

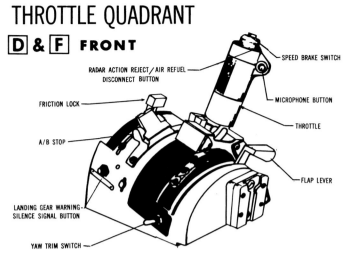

RADAR ACTION REJECT / AIR REFUEL DISCONNECT BUTTON

SPEED BRAKE SWITCH

FRICTION LOCK

MICROPHONE BUTTON

A/B STOP

THROTTLE

FLAP LEVER

LANDING GEAR WARNING SILENCE SIGNAL BUTTON

YAW TRIM SWITCH

F REAR

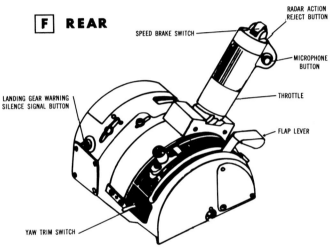

RADAR ACTION REJECT BUTTON

SPEED BRAKE SWITCH

MICROPHONE BUTTON

LANDING GEAR WARNING SILENCE SIGNAL BUTTON

THROTTLE

FLAP LEVER

YAW TRIM SWITCH

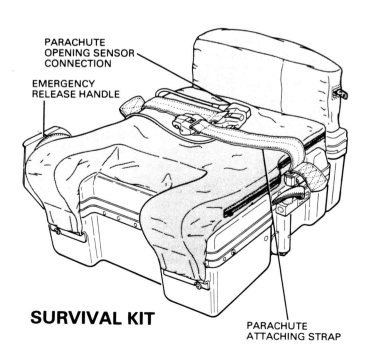

PARACHUTE OPENING SENSOR CONNECTION

EMERGENCY RELEASE HANDLE

SURVIVAL KIT

PARACHUTE ATTACHING STRAP

32

F-105 COLORS

Former Thunderbird Number 1, 57-814, as it appeared later in life with the 508th Tactical Fighter Group based at Hill AFB, Utah.

An F-105B in wrap-around camouflage as photographed at Hill AFB, in July 1980.

F-105Bs of the 466th TFS, 508th Group, use their cartridge starters during a "bare base" deployment at Biggs Army Airfield in December 1979.

Right and left side views of an F-105B of the New Jersey Air National Guard as displayed at an air show in March 1981.
(McMasters)

F-105D

This F-105D-10-RE, 60-475, with the Thunderstick II modification on the spine, belongs to the 457th TFS.
(Spidle)

F-105D-15-RE, 61-099, of the 465th TFS, Air Force Reserve, wears the map of Oklahoma on its tail.
(McMasters)

Another Reserve F-105D, this aircraft from the 466th TFS, appears to be in mint condition. *(McMasters)*

Two views of F-105D-25-RE, 61-167 from the Virginia Air National Guard which is stationed at Byrd Field near Richmond. These photographs were taken on November 11, 1979 while the aircraft was at Homestead AFB, Florida.
(Munkasy)

F-105D COCKPIT

Front instrument panel in an F-105D.

Left console showing throttles, control column, seat, and circuit breakers on the fuselage wall. Note that the throttle quadrant and handle are white. The right console is very similar to the right console in the front cockpit of the F-105G as shown on the next page.

F-105G FRONT COCKPIT

Front instrument panel and control column in an F-105G.

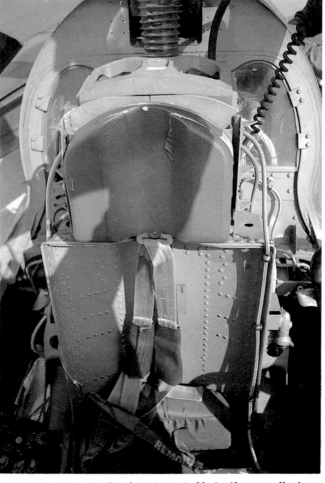

Looking back at the front seat. Note the small glass windows on either side of the seat. These provide only minimal forward visibility to the "Bear" in the back seat.

Left console detail in the front cockpit.

Right console and sidewall.

F-105G REAR COCKPIT

Above left: Rear instrument panel in an F-105G "Wild Weasel." Note the rear-view mirrors and radar scopes. There are a minimum of flight instruments, and the aircraft can be flown from the rear seat.
(Leader)

Above right: Close-up of the rear instrument panel.
(Leader)

Right: Looking rearward at the seat and canopy hinge mechanism in the rear cockpit.

Left console detail showing a gray throttle quadrant.

Right console and sidewall in the rear cockpit.

F-105D, F, G RADAR

Two views of the R-14 radar as used in the F-105D, -F, and -G.

F-105F

One of only two F-105Fs assigned to the Georgia ANG, as photographed in October 1981.

F-105F-1-RE, 63-8365, from the 465th TFS, as photographed in July 1980.   (McMasters)

F-105G

An F-105G, 63-8304, from George AFB, as it appeared in May 1977 on a visit to Holloman AFB, New Mexico.

Flying shot of F-105G, 63-8319, of the Georgia Air National Guard, on a training mission. The MER on the centerline carries six small practice bombs.
(Leader)

Another shot of 63-8319. The landing gear is down in preparation for landing.
(Leader)

63-8319 from below. This shot shows the wrap-around camouflage scheme and underside details to good advantage. Also note that the replacement main landing gear doors on the left side are not camouflaged.
(Leader)

DIMENSIONS

DIMENSION	ACTUAL	1/72nd SCALE	1/48th SCALE	1/32nd SCALE
Wingspan	34.9'	5.82"	8.73"	13.09"
Length (F-105B)	63.1'	10.52"	15.78"	23.66"
Length (F-105D)	64.4'	10.73"	16.10"	24.15"
Length (F-105F/G)	67.0'	11.17"	16.75"	25.13"
Height (F-105B/D)	19.7'	3.28"	4.93"	7.39"
Height (F-105F/G)	20.5'	3.42"	5.13"	7.69"
Wheel Tread	17.3'	2.88"	4.33"	6.49"

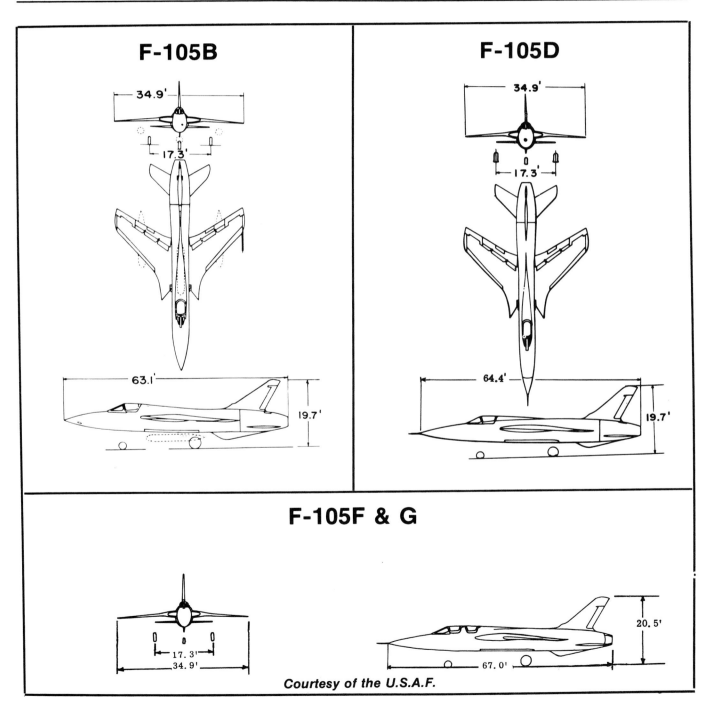

F-105B

F-105D

F-105F & G

Courtesy of the U.S.A.F.

F-105D THUNDERCHIEF

Five-view drawings of the F-105 and many other aircraft are available separately in 1/48th scale at a nominal price. Write to Aero Publishers, Inc., 329 West Aviation Road, Fallbrook, California 92028 for details.

DETAIL & SCALE, INC.

$\dfrac{1}{72 \text{ ND}}$ ──── SCALE

® FIVE-VIEW DRAWING

Terry G. Smith

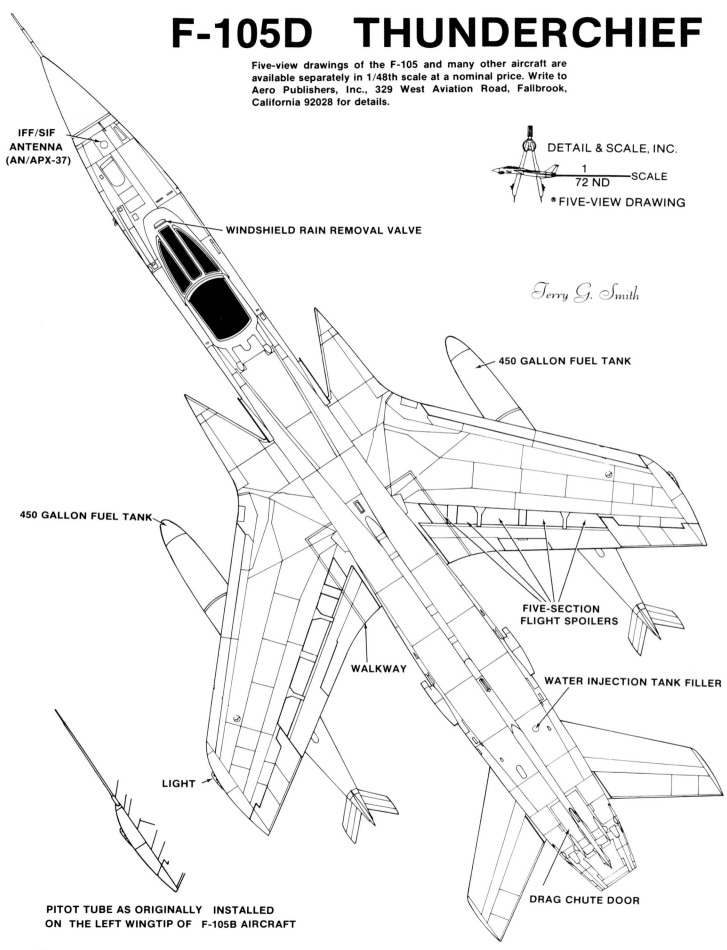

IFF/SIF ANTENNA (AN/APX-37)

WINDSHIELD RAIN REMOVAL VALVE

450 GALLON FUEL TANK

450 GALLON FUEL TANK

FIVE-SECTION FLIGHT SPOILERS

WALKWAY

WATER INJECTION TANK FILLER

LIGHT

DRAG CHUTE DOOR

PITOT TUBE AS ORIGINALLY INSTALLED ON THE LEFT WINGTIP OF F-105B AIRCRAFT

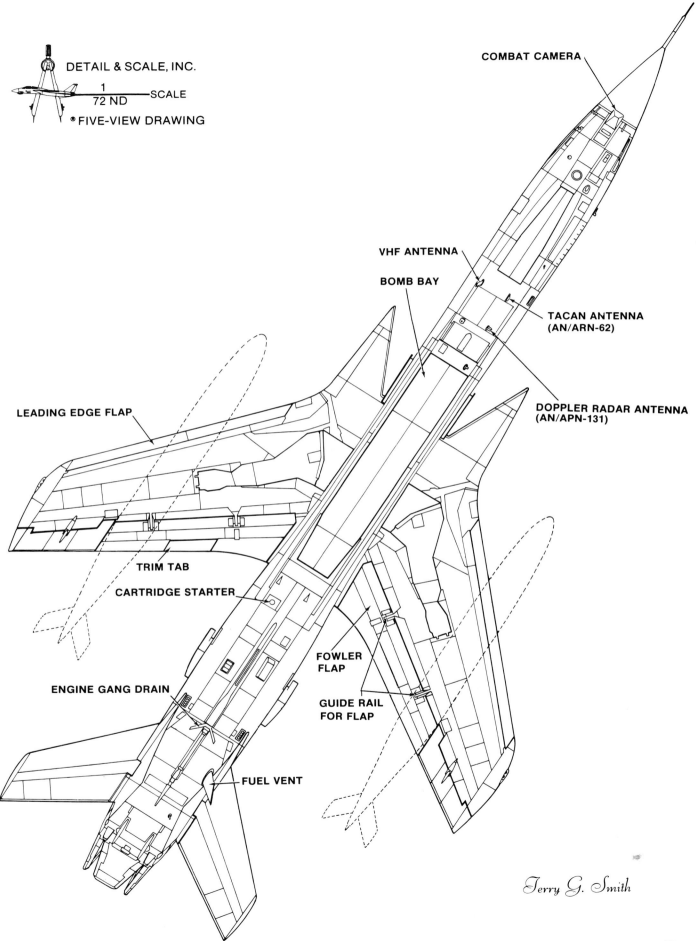

DETAIL & SCALE, INC.

$\frac{1}{72 \text{ ND}}$ SCALE

® FIVE-VIEW DRAWING

COMBAT CAMERA

VHF ANTENNA

BOMB BAY

TACAN ANTENNA
(AN/ARN-62)

LEADING EDGE FLAP

DOPPLER RADAR ANTENNA
(AN/APN-131)

TRIM TAB

CARTRIDGE STARTER

FOWLER
FLAP

ENGINE GANG DRAIN

GUIDE RAIL
FOR FLAP

FUEL VENT

Jerry G. Smith

43

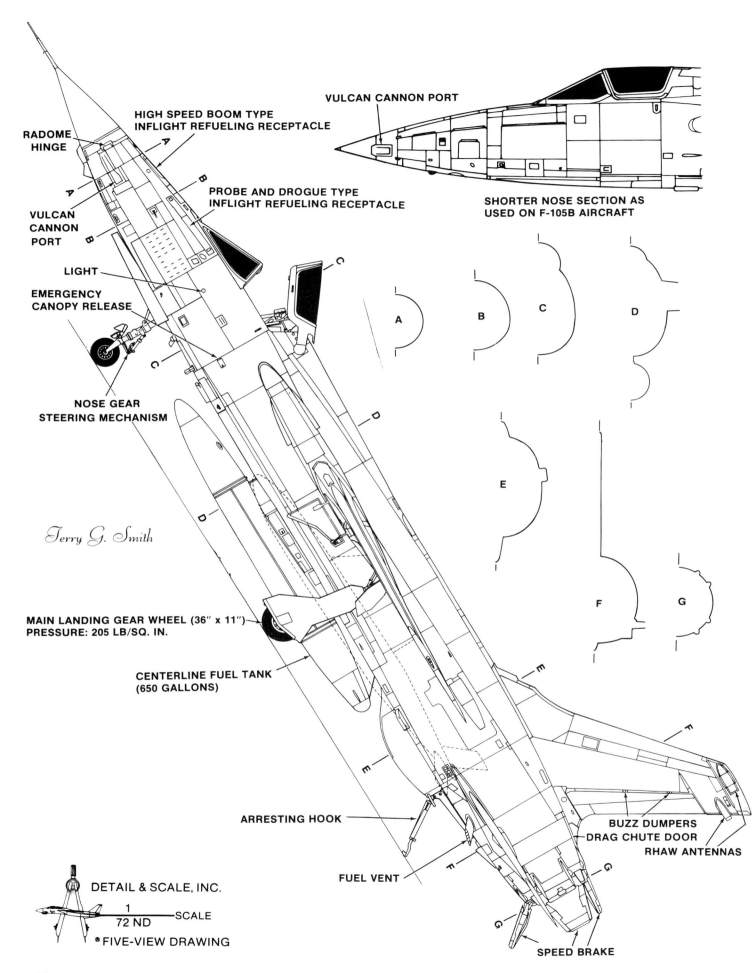

VULCAN CANNON PORT

SHORTER NOSE SECTION AS
USED ON F-105B AIRCRAFT

RADOME
HINGE

HIGH SPEED BOOM TYPE
INFLIGHT REFUELING RECEPTACLE

A

B

PROBE AND DROGUE TYPE
INFLIGHT REFUELING RECEPTACLE

VULCAN
CANNON
PORT

LIGHT

C

EMERGENCY
CANOPY RELEASE

C

NOSE GEAR
STEERING MECHANISM

D

D

A   B   C   D

E

Terry G. Smith

F   G

MAIN LANDING GEAR WHEEL (36″ x 11″)
PRESSURE: 205 LB/SQ. IN.

E

CENTERLINE FUEL TANK
(650 GALLONS)

E

F

ARRESTING HOOK

BUZZ DUMPERS

DRAG CHUTE DOOR

RHAW ANTENNAS

F

G

FUEL VENT

G

DETAIL & SCALE, INC.

1
————— SCALE
72 ND

® FIVE-VIEW DRAWING

G

SPEED BRAKE

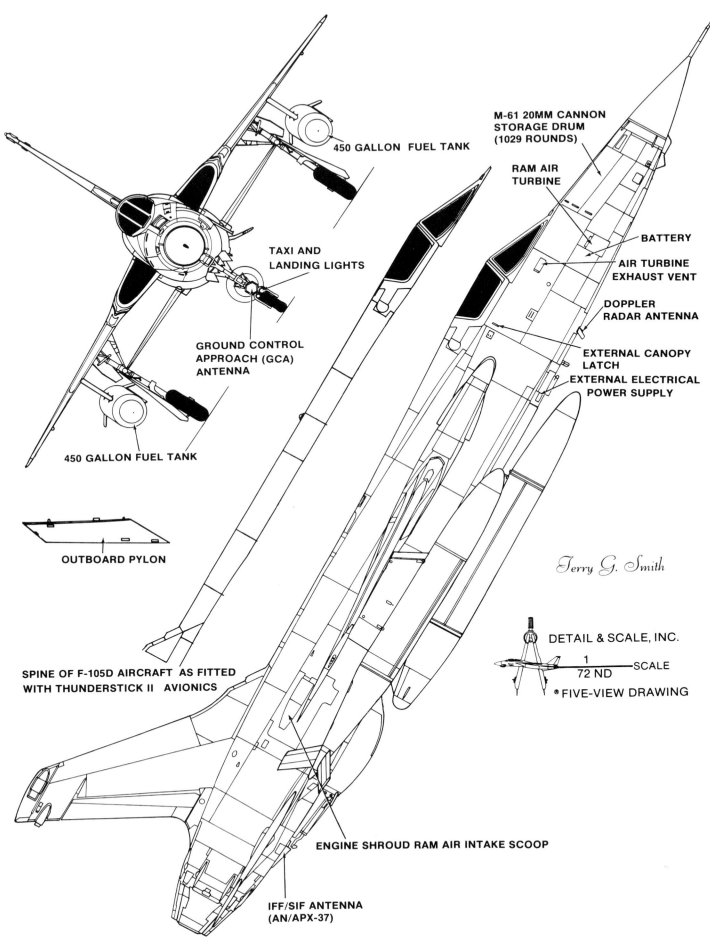

450 GALLON FUEL TANK

TAXI AND LANDING LIGHTS

GROUND CONTROL APPROACH (GCA) ANTENNA

450 GALLON FUEL TANK

OUTBOARD PYLON

SPINE OF F-105D AIRCRAFT AS FITTED WITH THUNDERSTICK II AVIONICS

M-61 20MM CANNON STORAGE DRUM (1029 ROUNDS)

RAM AIR TURBINE

BATTERY

AIR TURBINE EXHAUST VENT

DOPPLER RADAR ANTENNA

EXTERNAL CANOPY LATCH

EXTERNAL ELECTRICAL POWER SUPPLY

Jerry G. Smith

DETAIL & SCALE, INC.

$\dfrac{1}{72\text{ ND}}$ SCALE

® FIVE-VIEW DRAWING

ENGINE SHROUD RAM AIR INTAKE SCOOP

IFF/SIF ANTENNA (AN/APX-37)

45

F-105G "WILD WEASEL"

DETAIL & SCALE, INC.
$\frac{1}{72 \text{ ND}}$ SCALE
® FIVE-VIEW DRAWING

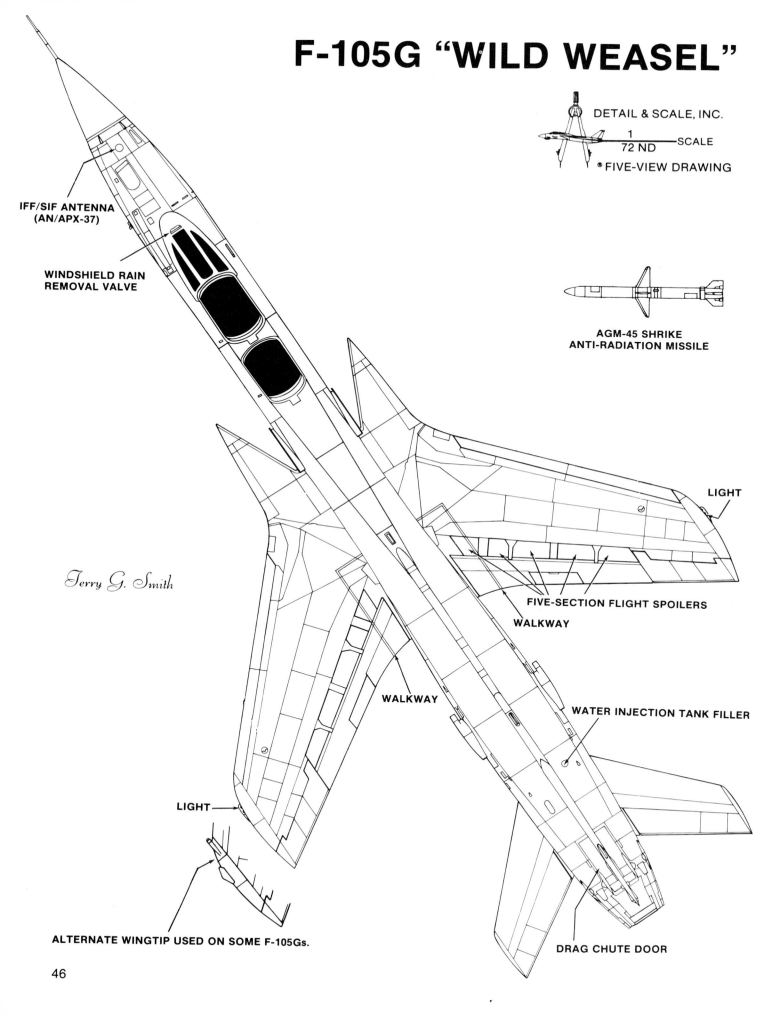

AGM-45 SHRIKE
ANTI-RADIATION MISSILE

IFF/SIF ANTENNA
(AN/APX-37)

WINDSHIELD RAIN
REMOVAL VALVE

Terry G. Smith

LIGHT

FIVE-SECTION FLIGHT SPOILERS

WALKWAY

WALKWAY

WATER INJECTION TANK FILLER

LIGHT

ALTERNATE WINGTIP USED ON SOME F-105Gs.

DRAG CHUTE DOOR

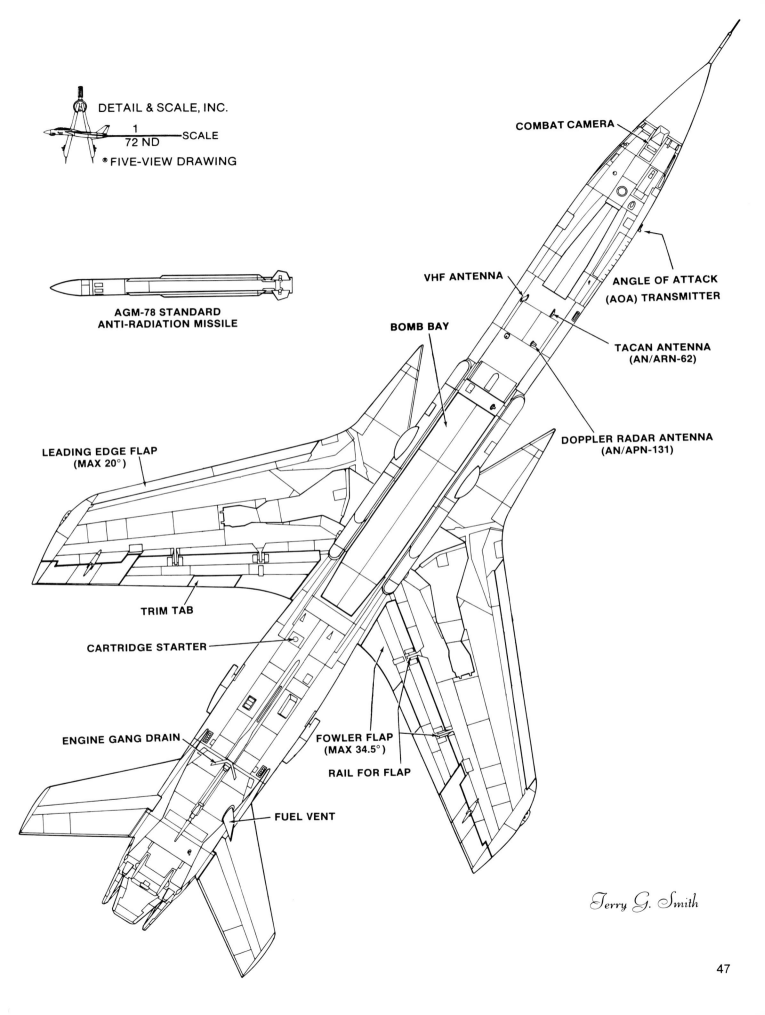

DETAIL & SCALE, INC.

$\dfrac{1}{72 \text{ ND}}$ SCALE

® FIVE-VIEW DRAWING

AGM-78 STANDARD
ANTI-RADIATION MISSILE

COMBAT CAMERA

VHF ANTENNA

BOMB BAY

ANGLE OF ATTACK
(AOA) TRANSMITTER

TACAN ANTENNA
(AN/ARN-62)

DOPPLER RADAR ANTENNA
(AN/APN-131)

LEADING EDGE FLAP
(MAX 20°)

TRIM TAB

CARTRIDGE STARTER

ENGINE GANG DRAIN

FOWLER FLAP
(MAX 34.5°)

RAIL FOR FLAP

FUEL VENT

Jerry G. Smith

47

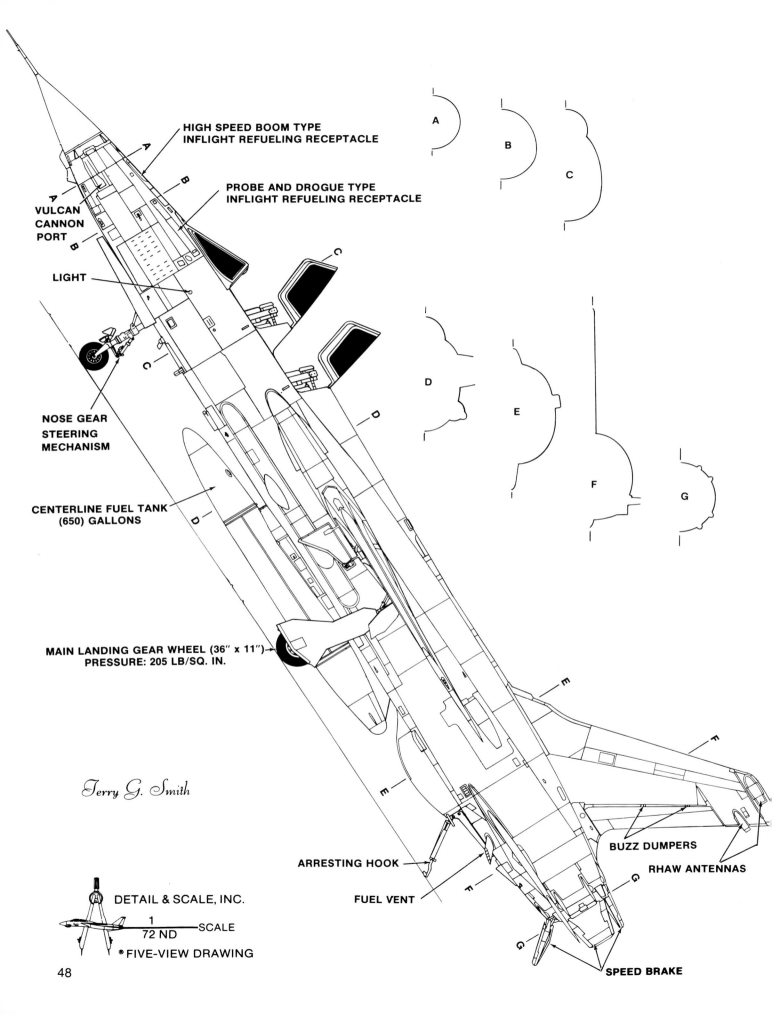

HIGH SPEED BOOM TYPE
INFLIGHT REFUELING RECEPTACLE

PROBE AND DROGUE TYPE
INFLIGHT REFUELING RECEPTACLE

VULCAN
CANNON
PORT

LIGHT

NOSE GEAR
STEERING
MECHANISM

CENTERLINE FUEL TANK
(650) GALLONS

MAIN LANDING GEAR WHEEL (36" x 11")
PRESSURE: 205 LB/SQ. IN.

Jerry G. Smith

ARRESTING HOOK

FUEL VENT

BUZZ DUMPERS

RHAW ANTENNAS

SPEED BRAKE

A

B

C

D

E

F

G

DETAIL & SCALE, INC.

$\frac{1}{72 \text{ ND}}$ SCALE

® FIVE-VIEW DRAWING

48

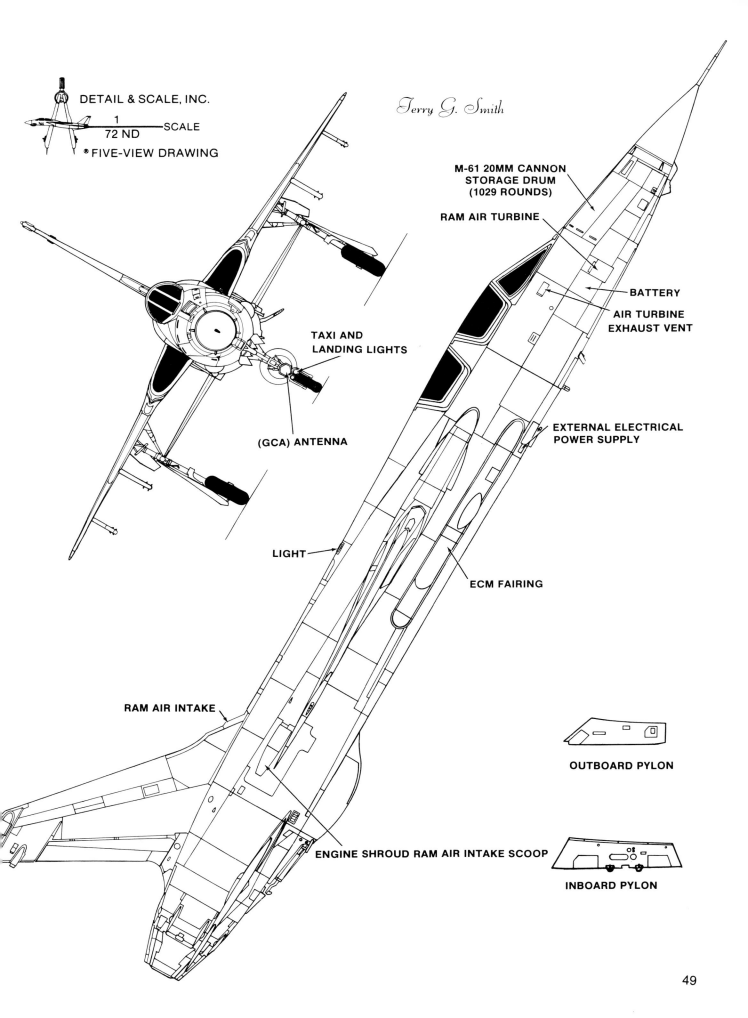

DETAIL & SCALE, INC.

$\dfrac{1}{72\ ND}$ ————SCALE

® FIVE-VIEW DRAWING

Terry G. Smith

M-61 20MM CANNON
STORAGE DRUM
(1029 ROUNDS)

RAM AIR TURBINE

BATTERY

AIR TURBINE
EXHAUST VENT

TAXI AND
LANDING LIGHTS

EXTERNAL ELECTRICAL
POWER SUPPLY

(GCA) ANTENNA

ECM FAIRING

LIGHT

OUTBOARD PYLON

RAM AIR INTAKE

INBOARD PYLON

ENGINE SHROUD RAM AIR INTAKE SCOOP

F-105F

Air Force Reserve F-105F-1-RE, 63-8261, of the 457th TFS, sports a map of its home state on its tail.(Cockle)

As mentioned earlier, the 143 F-105Fs produced were converted from the last F-105Ds ordered. The final acceptance of a two-seat F-105 came after the cancellation of two earlier proposed two-seat versions, the F-105C and F-105E.

The first flight of an F-105F was on June 11, 1963, and the aircraft exceeded the speed of sound. The first acceptance was at Nellis AFB on December 7, 1963, with initial operational service on December 23 of the same year. As with the F-105B and the -D before it, this first operational service was with the 4th Tactical Fighter Wing.

While the "Wild Weasel" work of the F-105F is well known, as is its later conversion to the F-105G, not so well known is its use in two other specialized roles. One such role was called Combat Martin, and for this mission F-105Fs were equipped with QRC-128 VHF jammers. Their purpose was to jam communications between the MiGs and their ground-control intercept facilities. Soviet tactics, followed by the North Vietnamese, usually called for the pilots to return to base when such communications were lost.

A second specialized modification fitted to a few F-105Fs was Commando Nail. This involved modifying the R-12 radar to give a sharper target resolu-

tion, and fitting the rear cockpit with a weapons release switch so that the rear seat pilot could take over that function. Thus equipped, these F-105s were used in dangerous night and bad weather low-level bombing missions. The first such mission was flown on April 26, 1967. These missions were later to be flown by the F-111.

Although a substantial number of war losses, and the conversion of about 60 more to F-105Gs, depleted the number of F-105Fs to a bare minimum, several examples served with the 508th Group and the Georgia Air National Guard until the last Thuds were retired.

F-105F-1-RE, 63-8343, in an early silver dope scheme. In this pre-war photo, note the lack of RHAW antennas on the tail and the lack of a combat camera under the nose. *(via I.A.A.P.)*

F-105F TECHNICAL DATA

Description

The principal mission of the F-105F is that of an all weather fighter-bomber. The aircraft has complete "one man" combat weapon system capability when flown from the forward cockpit with the additional capability of providing for an aft crew member. The primary purpose of the two-place F-105F is to provide a second cockpit for combat proficiency evaluation and transition training in an F-105 type aircraft.

The F-105F has a dual flight control capability and is distinguished from the F-105D by the two canopies, longer fuselage and a taller vertical tail. It is a thin midwing aircraft incorporating a bomb bay capable of housing a special store or an auxiliary fuel tank. It has dual air refueling capabilities, probe-drogue and boom receptacle. The wings are swept back and incorporate a spoiler/aileron combination for maneuvering at supersonic speeds as well as full span leading edge flaps and 3/4 span trailing edge flaps.

This aircraft is based on the F-105D-31 block and retains the same large store capacity and varied delivery methods in any weather. Combat mission execution is not dependent on an aft crewman, but complete nuclear blind capability can be accomplished in the aft cockpit. A transfer system allows either crew member to monitor or take control of all or any one system consisting of R-14 Search and Ranging Radar, Doppler Navigator and Compass, Automatic Flight Control System, Tacan, Communications and Weapons for efficient training or mission accomplishment. The Radar Doppler-Navigation systems permit accurate navigation to and from targets including a ground "hugging" terrain clearance mode in any weather from either cockpit.

DEVELOPMENT

The F-105F is a development of the earlier F-105D-31. The F-105F fuselage is 31 inches longer to accomodate second crew member and the vertical tail surface is increased 15%.

First flight	Jul 63
First operational use	Nov 63
CAT I test (completion)	Jul 64
CAT II test (completion)	Aug 64
Production completed	Dec 64

ELECTRONICS

Comm-Ident-Navig	AN/ASQ-37
UHF Command	AN/ARC-70
Direction Finder	AN/ARA-48
Marker Beacon	AN/ARN-61
Tacan	AN/ARN-62
IFF/SIF	AN/APX-37
Intercomm	AN/AIC-20
Doppler Navigation . . .	AN/APN-131
Fire Control System . . .	AN/ASG-19
RHAWS	AN/APR-25(V), -26(V)

GUNS

Nr	Type	Size	Rds ea	Location
1	M-61	20mm	1028	Fuselage

POWER PLANT

Nr & Model	(1) J75-P-19W
Mfr	Pratt & Whitney
Engine Spec Nr	A-2337-A
Type	Two Spool Axial
Length	259.3"
Diameter	43.0"
Weight (dry)	5950 lb
Augmentation .	Water & Afterburner
Tail Pipe . .	2-Position Convergent plus Republic Ram Air Ejector

ENGINE RATINGS

SLS	LB	-	RPM	-	MIN
T.O.	*26,500	-	6900/9090	-	2.5‡
Max:	†24,500	-	6400/8990	-	15
Mil:	16,100	-	6440/9000	-	30
Nor:	14,300	-	6080/8750	-	Cont

* With water and afterburner
† With afterburner operating
‡ Limited by water supply

WEIGHTS

Loading	LB	L.F.
Empty	30,419 (C)	
Basic	30,786 (C)	
Design . .	†35,812	8.67(7.33)
Combat . .	*38,738	
Max T.O. . .	54,580	
Max Land .	††51,727	

(C) Calculated
† No Store
* For Basic Mission
†† Limited by rate of sink
Note: Load factors in ( ) are for supersonic maneuvers.

FUEL

Location	Nr Tanks	Gal
Fuselage	7	†1160
Fus, bomb bay . . .	1	390
Wgs, ext, drop . . .	2	900
Fus, ext, drop . . .	1	*650
	Total	†3100
*450 (optional)	Total	†2900

† Includes 25 gal in tank lines

Grade JP-4
Specification MIL-J-5624

OIL

Engine, integral . . . 1 . . (tot) 4.5
Specification MIL-L-7808

WATER

Fus, aft . . . . 1 . . (tot) 36

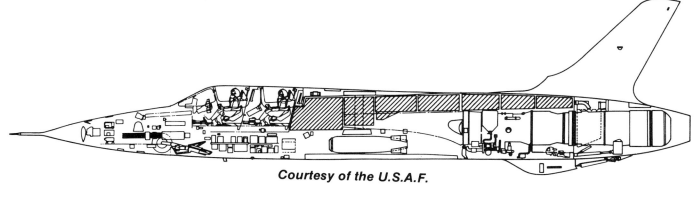

Courtesy of the U.S.A.F.

F-105F PERFORMANCE DATA

Loading and Performance—Typical Mission

CONDITIONS			BASIC MISSION I (S)	HI-LO-LO-HI II	HI-LO-LO-HI III	FERRY RANGE IV (S)
TAKE-OFF WEIGHT	(lb)		52,077	52,077	53,215	52,095
Fuel at 6.5 lb/gal (grade JP-4)	(lb)		16,907	16,907	15,119	19,344
Payload (Ammo)	(lb)		581	581	581	None
Payload (Bombs)	(lb)		1960 ⑤	1960 ⑤	4794 ⑥	None
Wing loading	(lb/sq ft)		135.3	135.3	138.2	135.3
Stall speed (power off)	(kn)		185.8	185.8	187.8	185.8
Take-off ground run at SL	(ft)	①	5490	5490	5825	5490
Take-off to clear 50 ft	(ft)	①	7770	7770	8260	7770
Rate of climb at SL	(fpm)	③	3650	3650	2500	3650
Time: SL to 20,000 ft	(min)	③	8.0	8.0	12.4	8.0
Time: SL to 30,000 ft	(min)	③	15.9	15.9	28.0 ⑦	15.9
Service ceiling (100 fpm)	(ft)	③	26,800	26,800	24,000	26,800
COMBAT RANGE	(n mi)		–	–	–	1300
COMBAT RADIUS	(n mi)		286(459) ⑧	537	386	518
Average cruise speed	(kn)		518	514	502	518
Initial cruising altitude	(ft)	②	26,400	26,400	19,500	26,400
Final cruising altitude	(ft)	②	34,000	34,000	34,000	34,000
Total mission time	(hr)	③	1.21	2.13	1.58	2.52
COMBAT WEIGHT	(lb)	②	38,738	40,081	38,121	33,964
Combat altitude	(ft)	②	S.L.	S.L.	S.L.	34,000
Combat speed	(kn)		681	673	694	848
Combat climb	(fpm)		25,500	21,700	25,900	10,100
Combat ceiling (500 fpm)	(ft)		45,100	43,800	45,500	47,800
Service ceiling (100 fpm)	(ft)		35,300	34,800	35,400	39,100
Max rate of climb at SL	(fpm)		25,500	21,700	25,900	29,100
Max speed at 36,000 ft	(kn)		773	672	797	848
Basic speed at SL	(kn/ft)		681	673	694	687
LANDING WEIGHT	(lb)		34,111	33,524	33,618	33,964
Ground roll at SL	(ft)		4860	4790	4800	4850
Ground roll (auxiliary brake)	(ft)	⑩	2670	2625	2630	2650
Total from 50 ft	(ft)		6700	6610	6625	6675
Total from 50 ft (auxiliary brake)	(ft)	⑩	4510	4440	4450	4490

① Take-off thrust with water injection
② Maximum thrust
③ Military thrust
④ DELETED
⑤ Internal Store
⑥ Six M-117, 750 lb bombs on C/L MER
⑦ Time to Climb to Service Ceiling
⑧ Wing tanks with 3870 lb of fuel are dropped prior to combat. Radius in ( ) is calculated carrying tanks in combat. F-105 Type II wing tanks are structurally compatible with external bombs which are carried in combat.

⑨⑩ With 20 ft diameter braking parachute
⑥⑦ Indicates performance for an instrument flight regulation climb schedule of 400 KCAS to optimum climb Mach Nr.
(S) MIL-C-5011A Mission

Courtesy of the U.S.A.F.

F-105F COCKPITS

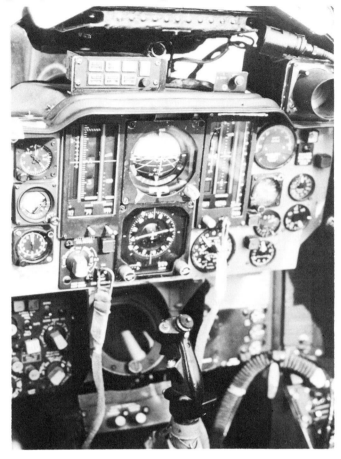

Above left: Front instrument panel in an F-105F.

Above right: Rear instrument panel in an F-105F.

Right: Right console in the rear cockpit of an F-105F. The right console in the front cockpit is the same as the F-105G shown on page 36.

Below left: Left console in the front cockpit.

Below right: Left console in the rear cockpit. Note that there are only minor differences between this console and the left console in the front cockpit.

All photos on this page are by Ray Leader.

F-105G "WILD WEASEL"

F-105G with the "Wild Weasel" WW on the tail. All F-105Gs were modified from F-105F airframes. This aircraft is from the 561st TFS.

While the F-105Fs that were modified for the "Wild Weasel" SAM suppression role proved effective, the Air Force ordered 60 F-105Fs to be further modified to increase their capability for this air defense suppression mission. Although the final number converted fell a few less than 60, there were 48 still in the inventory in 1973 when the United States ended all involvement. Only a handful were lost in combat performing this deadly mission, which attests to the effectiveness of both the aircraft and its crews.

In addition to the "Wild Weasel" modifications received by other -Fs, those converted to -G standards featured an internally mounted jamming system evidenced by the two pods faired into the sides of the lower fuselage. Extra sensing antennas on the wings, nose, and elsewhere enhanced the -G's capability to detect threats.

Although the F-105G was originally scheduled for a phase out of the active inventory in 1973, lack of a replacement aircraft prolonged its life for several years. Only when F-4G "Advanced Wild Weasels" were available in sufficient quantity were the -Gs sent to serve in the Air National Guard. The last unit to operate the F-105G was the Georgia Air National Guard at Dobbins AFB. Some of these proud veterans carried markings that were first applied in Vietnam even after being transferred to the Guard. They were the end of the line of an awesome looking fighter that served its nation proudly and well.

An F-105G "Wild Weasel" in a wrap-around camouflage scheme sits on the ramp at Nellis AFB awaiting Red Flag missions.
(Thurlow)

F-105G TECHNICAL DATA

Description

Courtesy of the U.S.A.F.

The principal mission of the F-105G is that of an all weather fighter-bomber. The F-105F aircraft is modified to an F-105G aircraft upon compliance with the following T.O.'s: 1F-105F-522, -522C, and -522D, "Installation of Improved Wild Weasel III Capability, 1F-105F-540, Installation of AN/ALR-31 Capability, 1F-105F-547, Installation of AGM-78B (Mod. 1) Capability, 1F-105F-548, 1F-105-550, Installation of ALQ-105 Capability, and 1F-105F-1079, Installation of QRL-373 Capability. The primary purpose of the two place F-105G is to provide an ECM capability.

The F-105G has a dual flight control capability and is distinguished from the F-105D by the two canopies, longer fuselage, and a taller vertical tail. It is a thin midwing aircraft incorporating a bomb bay capable of housing a special store or an auxilliary fuel tank. It has dual air refueling capabilities, probe-drogue and boom receptacle. The wings are swept back and incorporate a spoiler/aileron combination for maneuvering at supersonic speeds as well as full span leading edge flaps and 3/4 span trailing edge flaps.

The aircraft is based on the F-105F and retains the same large store capacity and varied delivery methods in any weather. However, unlike the F-105F, the F-105G has the Wild Weasel III Capability located throughout the aircraft providing radar homing and warning (RHAW) tape recorder and strike camera systems as well as an early warning missile site detection system. The F-105G also has the capability of carrying and launching the AGM-45A missiles from the outboard pylon stations as well as carrying and launching the AGM-78 missile from the inboard pylon stations.

POWER PLANT

Nr & Model	(1) J75-P-19W
Mfr	Pratt & Whitney
Engine Spec Nr	A-2337-A
Type	Two Spool Axial
Length	259.3"
Diameter	43.0"
Weight (dry)	5950 lb
Augmentation	Water & Afterburner
Tail Pipe	2-Position Convergent plus Republic Ram Air Ejector

ENGINE RATINGS

SLS	LB	-	RPM	-	MIN
T.O.	*26,500	-	6900/9090	-	2.5‡
Max:	†24,500	-	6400/8990	-	15
Mil:	16,100	-	6440/9000	-	30
Nor:	14,300	-	6080/8750	-	Cont

* With water and afterburner
† With afterburner operating
‡ Limited by water supply

ELECTRONICS

Comm-Ident-Navig	AN/ASQ-37
UHF Command	AN/ARC-70
Direction Finder	AN/ARA-48
Marker Beacon	AN/ARN-61
Tacan	AN/ARN-62
IFF/SIF	AN/APX-37
Intercomm	AN/AIC-20
Doppler Navigation	AN/APN-131
Fire Control System	AN/ASG-19
RHAWS	AN/APR-35, -36, -37
RHAWS	AN/ALR-31
ECM	AN/ALQ-105
ECM	AN/ALT-34

Wing

Span	34.9'
Incidence (root)	0°
(tip)	0°
Cathedral	3°30'
Sweepback (25% Chord)	45°
Wing Area	385 sq ft
Aspect Ratio	3.18
M. A. C.	137.76 in

Wing Section
(root - Sta 80) . . NACA 65A-005.5
(tip) . . . . . . NACA 65A-003.7

WEIGHTS

Loading	LB	L.F.
Empty	31,279 (C)	
Basic	31,646 (C)	
Design	†35,812	8.67 (7.33)
Combat	*41,091	
Max T.O.	54,580	
Max Land.	††51,727	

(C) Calculated
† No Store
* For Basic Mission
†† Limited by rate of sink
Note: Load factors in ( ) are for supersonic maneuvers.

FUEL

Location	Nr Tanks	Gal
Fuselage	7	†1051
Fus, bomb bay	1	375
Wgs, ext, drop	2	900
Fus, ext, drop	1	*650
	Total:	†2976

* 450 (optional) . . . . Total: *2776
†Includes 25 gal in tank lines

Grade	JP-4
Specification	MIL-J-5624

OIL

Engine, integral . . 1	(tot) 4.5
Specification	MIL-L-7808

WATER

Fus, aft 1	(tot) 36

GUNS

Nr	Type	Size	Rds ea	Location
1	M-61	20mm	1028	Fuselage

F-105G, 63-275, of the Georgia Air National Guard taxis out for a training mission.   *(Leader)*

F-105G PERFORMANCE DATA

Loading and Performance—Typical Mission

CONDITIONS		BASIC MISSION I (S)	HI-LO-LO-HI II	HI-LO-LO-HI III	FERRY RANGE IV (S)
TAKE-OFF WEIGHT [12]	(lb)	53,111	53,111	54,580	52,962
Fuel at 6.5 lb/gal(grade JP-4)	(lb)	16,419	16,419	19,344	19,344
Payload (Ammo)	(lb)	581	581	581	None
Payload (Bombs)	(lb)	2180 [5]	2130 [5]	776 [6]	None
Wing loading	(lb/sq ft)	138.0	138.0	141.8	137.6
Stall speed (power off)	(kn)	187.6	187.6	190.2	187.3
Take-off ground run at SL	(ft)	5800	5800	6255	5740
Take-off to clear 50 ft	(ft)	8210	8210	8270	8100
Rate of climb at SL	(fpm)	2900	2900	2800	3400
Time: SL to 20,000 ft	(min)	12.4	12.4	12.4	10.4
Time: SL to 30,000 ft [7]	(min)	28.0	28.0	32.0	22.7
Service ceiling (100 fpm) [3]	(ft)	24,600	24,600	23,300	24,600
COMBAT RANGE	(n mi)	-	-	-	1271
COMBAT RADIUS	(n mi)	391	441	591	
Average cruise speed	(kn)	514	515	514	518
Initial cruising altitude	(ft)	24,000	24,000	23,000	25,400
Final cruising altitude	(ft)	33,200	32,600	33,500	33,800
Total mission time	(hr)	1.62	1.76	2.35	2.47
COMBAT WEIGHT	(lb)	41,091	39,833	41,327	34,948
Combat altitude	(ft)	S.L.	S.L.	S.L.	33,800
Combat speed	(kn)	681	681	684	706
Combat climb	(fpm)	23,000	23,400	22,800	9400
Combat ceiling (500 fpm)	(ft)	43,900	44,200	43,500	46,800
Service ceiling (100 fpm)	(ft)	34,800	35,000	34,800	38,400
Max rate of climb at SL	(fpm)	23,000	23,400	22,800	27,100
Max speed at 36,000 ft	(kn)	723	706	729	706
Basic speed at SL	(kn/ft)	681	681	684	674
LANDING WEIGHT	(lb)	35,266	34,519	34,519	34,948
Ground roll at SL	(ft)	5010	4920	4920	4970
Ground roll (auxiliary brake)	(ft)	2760	2700	2700	2740
Total from 50 ft	(ft)	6890	6770	6770	6840
Total from 50 ft (auxiliary brake)	(ft)	4630	4560	4560	4600

NOTES

1 Take-off thrust with water injection
2 Maximum thrust
3 Military thrust
4 DELETED
5 1 AGM-78 (R.I.B.) and 2 AGM-45's (O.B.)
6 2 AGM-45's (O.B.)
7 Time to Climb to Service Ceiling
8 With 20 ft diameter braking parachute
13 Indicates performance for an instrument flight regulation climb schedule of 400 KCAS to optimum climb Mach Nr.
S MIL-C-5011A Mission

F-105G ORDNANCE

AGM-45 Shrike missile mounted on the outboard right pylon.

AGM-78 Standard ARM on the inboard left pylon. (USAF)

Shrike and Standard ARMs carried together under the right wing. (Leavitt)

Six 500 pound high drag "Snakeye" bombs on the centerline pylon of an F-105G. (Leavitt)

Two views of an AGM-78 Standard ARM on the centerline pylon on an F-105G.

F-105G WALK-AROUND

Top of the nose on an F-105G. The lighter colored panel is the high-speed boom in-flight refueling receptacle. (Malerba)

Cannon muzzle detail on the left side of the nose. Also note the combat camera located under the nose, the triangular antenna, and the radome hinge.

Cannon barrels of the M-61 20mm Vulcan cannon in an F-105G. All F-105s carried the Vulcan. (Leader)

Cannon breech and rotator assembly of the Vulcan cannon. (Leader)

Cannon bay open with the cannon removed.

Open panels just below and behind the cannon on the left side of the nose. The larger panel at the right is the left hydraulics bay.

Electronics compartment on the left side.

Cooling scoop for avionics compartments. Note the light on the scoop, and the Westinghouse ALQ-105 fairings on the sides.
(Malerba)

Photographs of the afterburner cooling scoop added to both sides of the fuselage to all F-105s after some early engine fires were experienced.

Speed brake detail. The sections of the speed brake are known as petals. Note the open parabrake housing at the base of the vertical tail. (Thurlow)

Right side of the vertical stabilizer on an F-105G. The F-105F and F-105G had a taller tail than the F-105B or -D, and it was also broader in chord. This increase in chord is particularly noticeable near the base of the leading edge.

Open panels under the right rear fuselage.

Flap detail on the right wing.

Wing tip detail of an F-105G showing the extra antenna added for the Wild Weasel role. The antenna is no longer used, and is being deleted. (Malerba)

Westinghouse ALQ-105 pod on the right side. Looking for this pod is the easiest way to tell an F-105G from an F-105F.

Electronics compartments on the right side.

Air turbine unit (top), with the battery below. To the left of the battery is the right hydraulics bay. Note the exhaust for the air turbine unit.

Ram air turbine in the open position.

Right side of the nose of an F-105G showing the combat camera and two of the four triangular antennas just behind the radome.

MODELER'S SECTION

KIT REVIEWS

1/144th SCALE KIT

Otaki 1/144th Scale F-105D, Number OT2-20

This is the smallest model available of the Thunderchief, and it is quite good. The scribing is of the recessed type, and is very complete with RHAW antennas on the tail and a combat camera under the nose.

The cockpit area is plugged, and no details are provided. However, it is easily opened and detailed if the individual modeler so desires. Centerline and inboard wing pylons are provided, each with an external fuel tank attached, but no outer wing pylons are provided. However, these are easily constructed from plastic stock. Likewise, the saber drain, located under the left rear fuselage and missing from the kit, should be added from thin stock.

If you have never built a model in 1/144th scale, particularly a small one of a fighter, this is one you really should try. We recommend this model.

1/100th SCALE KIT

Tamiya 1/100th Scale F-105D, Number PA1026

Moving up one notch in size over the Otaki 1/144th scale kit, this model is also an excellent replica of the F-105D. It shows the combat improvements made to the Thud, such as RHAW antennas, combat camera, and afterburner cooling scoops.

Surface detailing is a combination of both the recessed and raised type, and again is quite accurate and complete. The cockpit detail consists of a seat and partial floor, so extra detailing will be desirable. As a minimum, an instrument panel should be added. Landing gear wheels, struts, and doors are nicely done, but the main gear wells lack detail, and the nose well is plugged. Like the Otaki kit, the saber drain is missing and should be added.

Centerline and inboard and outboard wing pylons are provided with MERs attached to the centerline and inboard wing pylons. 750 pound bombs are pro-

Otaki 1/144th scale F-105D.

(Schmenk)

Tamiya 1/100th scale F-105D.   *(Schmenk)*

vided for the MERs and single bombs are provided for the outboard pylons.

With a little work and detailing, this kit can be built into a very nice model. We recommend this model, but it is no longer generally available.

1/72nd SCALE KITS

Revell 1/72nd F-105, Number H-231

While this kit is not exactly 1/72nd scale, it really isn't any scale. It measures one scale in one direction, and another scale in another direction. But it is close to 1/72nd scale, so it is being covered here under 1/72nd scale kits.

The model was the first released of the Thud, and shows its age which dates back to 1957. It has a working in-flight refueling door, and proportions and shapes are questionable at best. As examples, the air intakes are too small and have the wrong sweep, and the pylons do not represent any pylons ever carried by the F-105. The four bombs look something like 3000 pounders, but are too small and not correctly proportioned.

The cockpit consists of a seat and a pilot figure, and interestingly enough the small windows behind the canopy are provided. These windows were only present on the early prototypes, so this feature indicates that Revell must have used one of these prototypes as the subject of its model.

With a lack of detail, and with molding that is less than crisp and delicate, this model just does not look right when finished. There are better kits of both the F-105B and F-105D available.

Monogram 1/72nd Scale F-105, Number 6808

Like the Revell kit, this is one of the older kits of the F-105. Some analysis of the kit indicates that Monogram also used a prototype or test aircraft as its

subject. The model represents a short-nosed Thud, so it has to be a -B model or older. But it also comes with a probe on the nose, and of the short-nosed versions only the test aircraft had these probes. However, the small windows behind the canopy are not present, so one of the first two prototypes can be ruled out. This means that one of the thirteen YF-105Bs was probably the subject.

While definitely a short nosed F-105, the box art shows a radome painted on the aircraft that is about the size of the one used on the -D. The instructions state that the model is an F-105D. However this simply is not the case. It comes fairly close to being one of those test aircraft.

Surface detailing consists mostly of lines of rivets which are grossly oversize. These should be sanded down. The cockpit consists of a floor and consoles, and a seat with the pilot molded in place. The canopy and windscreen is nicely molded, and has squared corners making it more accurate than the ones in the Hasegawa/Minicraft kits which are too rounded. We used two canopies and one windscreen from this kit in building our F-105F conversion. The straight top line to the canopy made it the only one acceptable, especially for the rear cockpit.

Landing gear struts are quite crude and lack detail. Wheel wells are non-existent. Pylons, bombs, and fuel tanks simply are not accurate. But by using the fuselage, reworking the wings, and adding parts such as landing gear, horizontal tails, and smaller detail parts from a Hasegawa or Minicraft kit, it would be interesting to see the result of an effort to model one of the early test aircraft.

It should also be noted that, for the purpose of a diorama, a ground crewman is provided which is useable, as is a boarding ladder which is not. But this kit is in no way in the same class as Monogram's new F-105G in 1/48th scale.

Minicraft 1/72nd F-105D with a Thunderstick II modification on the spine. **(Schmenk)**

Hasegawa/Minicraft 1/72nd Scale F-105D, Number JS-014

This -D version has been released twice (but not molded) in the United States by Minicraft. The -B version (covered next) has been molded by Minicraft in the United States. It has also been released by AMT as kit number A656.

This is one of Hasegawa's older kits, and while not as beautifully detailed as some of their latest releases, it is still the best F-105D in 1/72nd scale. As stated above, the kit has been released twice, and the second version was updated by the addition of afterburner cooling intakes and RHAW antennas for the tail. It is really nice to see a company pay attention to update details such as these, and we wish more companies would do some simple retooling to their molds when re-releasing kits. In addition to these changes, the new release had different decals.

This model of the F-105D, which is the only -D available in 1/72nd scale, is generally accurate in dimension and outline. About the only really noticeable problem in this area is the canopy which is too rounded. Surface detailing is good, consisting of finely scribed recessed lines and a few rivets. However, a noticeable omission is the series of gun gas vents on the left side of the nose.

Landing gear struts are delicate, and care must be taken to properly line up the main gear or a noticeable "toe-out" problem will result with the main wheels. There is no nose gear well, and the sides of the main gear wells are open. Serious modelers will probably want to fill these in with card stock.

A centerline fuel tank is provided, and a pylon and ECM pod is also supplied for this station. We recommend using the fuel tank, or replacing it with an MER and bombs from another kit. For the wing pylons, fuel tanks are provided for the inboard pylons, and Bullpups are included for the outboard pylons. Better Bullpups can be found in the Minicraft A-4 kit, but again, bombs or ECM pods would be better suited for these pylons. If Bullpups are carried, they will require an appropriate launch rail.

The pylons themselves have some heavy scribing, and some round mold marks, and these should be sanded off.

Cockpit detail is rather sparse by today's standards, consisting of a pilot figure molded into a seat, which is in turn glued to a floor/seat back combination. A decal instrument panel is also provided. With all the space available, most modelers may want to add more detail. A combat camera should also be added to the nose.

While not up to the excellent standard of recent Hasegawa releases, this is still a very good kit, and most shortcomings are simply a matter of the kit being one that is over ten years old. We recommend this kit as being the best in 1/72nd scale.

Two views of an F-105D from Minicraft in 1/72nd scale.

Minicraft/Hasegawa 1/72nd Scale F-105B, Numbers 122 and 1014

Originally this kit was produced by Hasegawa in Japan, and then packaged and sold in the United States by Minicraft as kit 122. Later, Minicraft produced the kit in the United States under license as kit 1014. The differences between the two were the markings and the box. We will treat these two releases in one review.

This kit is directly decended from the Hasegawa F-105D covered above. New fuselage halves with the shorter nose are provided, and the original pitot probe on the left wing tip has been added. Everything else remains the same as with the -D kit. The original reason for making the -B was to complete the collection of "Thunderbird" aircraft, and it is these markings that appear in kit 122. Kit 1014 has markings for an F-105B of the 335th TFS, 4th TFW, which include green bands on the nose and tail, and the familiar "chief's head" insignia. This is noteworthy because this same scheme was used on -Bs and -Ds, and can easily be adapted for both versions. But two words of caution are necessary here. The number and markings supplied on the Scale-Master sheet included in the kit are correct for an F-105B-15-RE. However the instructions in the kit show an F-105D. Follow the box art for correct placement. This brings up the second word of caution. The box art shows the fuel tanks attached to the outboard wing pylons, and the Bullpups attached to the inboard pylons. This is backward. Fuel tanks cannot be carried on the outboard pylons. Only the inboard and centerline pylons are "wet".

All other comments in the F-105D review apply to this kit. We recommend this kit as the best available of the F-105B.

Airfix/MPC 1/72nd Scale F-105G, Number 1-4408

The fit of this kit is generally good, with some filling and sanding needed at the wing roots and where the afterburner can joins the aft fuselage. However, the fit of the clear parts is very poor.

Although the raised panel lines are crisply molded, they are too heavy for this scale. In the cockpit, raised lines are used to detail the consoles and instrument panels, and this detailing is generally inaccurate. It falls far short of that provided in the Monogram 1/72nd scale F-105F/G kit. The control columns and seats are also not very accurate, and should be replaced.

The wheel wells have some raised detail in the form of bracing only. No lines, plumbing, or connectors are present. There are no walls to the main gear wells, so what you come up with is not very realistic. When

MPC 1/72nd scale F-105G.

assembled, the nose gear doors are too far away from the bottom of the fuselage, leaving a very noticeable gap. The nose gear strut leaves something to be desired when it comes to accuracy and detailing. The main gear struts also lack detail, and are very flimsy. They tend to wobble when the weight of the model is placed on them.

The same stores provided in the Monogram 1/48th scale F-105G are included here, consisting of two Shrikes, a Standard ARM, one 450 gallon wing tank, and a 650 gallon centerline tank. The missiles are lacking in detail when compared to the Monogram kit. The centerline tank is too short, is incorrectly shaped, and has the wrong taper at the front. The fins on the tank are incorrect in size.

Clear parts are too thick, but they are clear. They are too narrow and too high. This is particularly true for the windscreen. The framing is too thick, and they fit very poorly.

The biggest problem with this kit is its shape and proportions. The vertical tail is incorrect for an F-105F or -G, being the shorter tail with a more narrow chord as used on single seat F-105s. The horizontal stabilators are too wide in chord at the root, and this causes them to have too much taper and sweepback. The burner can is too blunt, and has actuators that are way too large. The vertical fin under the tail is the wrong shape at the leading edge. The nose is too wide, being noticeably fat and thick.

RHAW antennas, common to the F-105G version, are missing from the nose and wing tips. The tail hook is also missing. In short, this model is not as well researched or molded as the Monogram kit in 1/72nd scale. In our estimation, it is not up to the standard of most Airfix kits of the past ten years.

Model built and reviewed by Alan Toon. Sample courtesy of Historical Hobbies, Doraville, Georgia.

Monogram 1/72nd Scale F-105F/G, Number 5431

Detail and Scale received a test shot of this model

Monogram 1/72nd scale F-105G. This new kit is the best 1/72nd scale F-105 presently available on the market. **(Monogram)**

just prior to press time for the second printing of this book. The lack of time prevented us from building the model, but close examination reveals that the kit is really excellent. It is simply a scaled-down version of the earlier Monogram F-105G in 1/48th scale. Although a lot smaller than its 1/48th scale brother, this kit loses little if any of the superb detailing found in the bigger kits. Cockpit detailing is scribed into the instrument panels and consoles, and the ejection seats have belts, buckles, and handles all molded in place. Even the tiny control columns are well detailed. In short, this is easily one of the best detailed cockpits we have seen in a 1/72nd scale kit. Usually, only 1/48th and larger scale kits have all of the extras found in this model, and this is likely a result of Monogram scaling down the many nice details found on their 1/48th scale F-105G. If this is the result of a kit manufacturer doing a scale-down of an existing larger kit, it makes us wish that all 1/72nd scale kits were the results of such a scale-down. Unfortunately, most 1/72nd scale kits, designed as such from the start, do not have anywhere near this much detail.

As with the cockpits, the landing gear and wheel wells are also extensively detailed. All sorts of plumbing, lines, connectors, fittings, and braces are visible in both the main gear and nose gear wells.

Surface scribing is the raised type, and is very delicate. External stores are the same as found in the 1/48th scale F-105G kit covered below. All other features also parallel that kit, to include the lower speed brake petal hanging in the down position, and the gun barrel piece to go inside the open muzzle is likewise present. After seeing this kit, along with the EF-111A kit that Monogram has just released, we are glad to see new 1/72nd scale kits from this company. This

F-105G is clearly the best 1/72nd scale model available of the Thud. We recommend this kit very highly, and we hope to see Monogram do an equally impressive 1/72nd scale F-105D.

1/48th SCALE KITS

Monogram 1/48th Scale F-105G, Number 5806-0610

In our estimation, this is the best kit available of any version of the Thunderchief in any scale. It is accurate, detailed, and beautifully molded. It may well be the best 1/48th scale model that Monogram has produced.

Impressive by its large size, it is also equally impressive by its attention to tiny detail. The surface scribing is very delicate and absolutely accurate. Even the small ribs in the air turbine exhaust vent, and a similar vent on the left side, are reproduced.

Detail abounds, and would take many pages to cover completely. The cockpit has beautiful consoles with every switch in place. The fuselage sides have appropriate panels molded on them. Auxillary panels, throttle quadrants, and seat belts on accurately detailed seats are all included. The control columns are beautiful, but the one lacking detail seems to be the throttle handles. We could not find these on the test shot. Both front and rear instrument panels have all instruments, knobs, and switches beautifully molded in.

The landing gear is excellent. The struts are accurately molded with lights and hydraulic lines, and the nose strut is split vertically from top to bottom. This makes for a stronger, more accurate strut with the proper fork design. The doors are equally detailed with hydraulic lines and other details. The wells contain details too - everywhere! The nose gear well is a separate box with lines, cylinders, and piping molded in. The main gear wells have details molded in on several pieces. There is a separate wing spar with details at the rear of the wells. The bottoms of the top wings have the appropriate ribs. The inboard well detail is molded on the fuselage sides, and the lower wings have the walls and remaining well details included. When all assembled, these parts formed the most detailed and accurate wheel wells ever included in a scale model kit.

The speed brake petals are all separate pieces, with the lower petal hanging down at the proper angle. The interior of each intake is molded to the fuselage side so that no inaccessable seams result inside the intakes. This shows a lot of thought on the part of the people responsible for engineering this model. The gun muzzle is open, and a piece with the six barrel

Monogram 1/48th scale F-105G.

ends is included to fit inside the hole. This gives the appearance that the Vulcan cannon is in place in the model.

The Westinghouse jamming pods are separate pieces, making conversion to an -F simple. Just leave off the pods, remove the four triangular antennas around the nose, remove the antennas from the wing tips, and presto, you have an F-105F. But surely Monogram will re-release this kit as an -F, and hopefully as a -D in the future. Indeed, a -B could also easily be made in the same way Hasegawa changed their -D to a -B.

External ordnance is an interesting mix. There is a centerline fuel tank, and another external tank for one of the inboard wing pylons. The other inboard wing pylon carries a Standard ARM, and Monogram correctly used the weapon pylon for the Standard (complete with launch rail), and used the different fuel tank pylon with the external tank. This provides different options, particularly when one has two kits and supplements with stores from other models. Two Shrike missiles are provided for the outboard wing pylons.

The model has lots of little extras, like reinforcing strips molded on the wings, and the model lends itself well to extra detailing if desired. An open radome, gun bay, or other access panels would make this model even more impressive. Easily, this is the best model of the Thunderchief that is available.

Monogram 1/48th Scale F-105F, Number 5808

This kit is essentially a re-release of the F-105G reviewed above. The Westinghouse ALQ-105 fairings have been removed, and the ordnance load has been changed. Now included are two 450 gallon wing tanks, two five-hundred pound bombs with fuse extenders, and six 750 pound bombs, with two having extenders and four without extenders. A multiple ejector rack is provided to carry the six 750 pound bombs on the centerline station.

Monogram correctly changed the outboard pylons from the type used to carry Shrike missiles (as used in the F-105G kit) to the type used for bombs and other ordnance. But this, along with the deletion of the ALQ-105 fairings, is the extent of the changes made. They should have also removed the four small triangular shaped antennas around the nose since these were not present on standard F-105Fs. Likewise, the RHAW antennas on the wing tips should have been removed. Fortunately, the modeler can make these changes himself with little effort.

If an early F-105F is to be modeled, the RHAW antennas on the vertical tail will also have to be removed. Sanding off the one on the trailing edge will not be too difficult, but the one on the tip will be harder. In sanding it off, the modeler will go through the plastic and a hole will result. This will then need to be

Monogram 1/48th scale F-105F.

(Monogram)

filled and sanded smooth. The markings supplied by Monogram for this kit are for such an early -F, so if these markings are to be used, the modeler should be sure to remove all of these antennas. Finally, the combat camera under the nose should also be removed if an early -F is modeled.

Monogram provided a shark's mouth marking for this model. This marking was used by the 23rd TFW on its F-105s during the time the aircraft were painted with a protective silver paint. This marking was carried on that unit's F-105D's, but there is no indication that it was ever carried on an F-105F. We do not believe it is accurate for an F-105F.

The rest of the kit is the same as the F-105G covered above. Review comments for that kit apply here. Like that model, this one is also excellent, and we recommend this model. Now - if Monogram would only do a 1/48th scale F-105D!

1/32nd SCALE KIT

Combat Models 1/32nd Scale F-105D & F, Number 32-023

Combat Models has a reputation of producing vacu-formed models that are impressive in both size and quality. This model of the Thunderchief is no exception. This kit has been released twice, the first time with two fuselages, one for the -D and one for the -F, but the second release includes only one fuselage. However, instructions explain how to modify it to build either version. Another change is the deletion of the horizontal stabilators which were included in the first release. In the second release a .60 plastic card is supplied from which the stabilators are to be made. Since large 1/32nd scale drawings come with the kits, this is no problem.

The kit is nicely molded with good surface details. There are even reinforcing strips under the wings. The speed brake petals are molded separately, and vertical tails for both the -D and -F are provided. Clear canopy and windscreen parts are likewise provided for both versions. Some small parts such as wheels are also provided, but, as with most vacu-formed models, the modeler must supply a lot of detail on his own. But with a lot of work and patience, this kit provides the basis for a real museum piece. We recommend this kit for the experienced modeler.

Any modeler not familiar with Combat Models, and desiring more information on their line, should write to:

Combat Models
1633 Marconi Road
Wall, New Jersey 07719

Combat Models 1/32nd scale vacu-formed model. This model can be built as a -D, -F, or -G. The little model is the Otaki 1/144th scale kit.

(Schmenk)

DECAL SUMMARY

Note: It is impossible to completely review decals unless the reviewer has actually used the decals on a model to see how they fit. Additionally, markings on a given aircraft can be changed from time to time, so it is possible that the decals may be accurate for one point in time and not another. Therefore, this section is more of a listing of decals available than a review. Review comments are made only in regard to fit when we have actually used the decals or as to accuracy when the evidence clearly indicated an error.

1/144th SCALE KITS

Otaki Kit Number OT2-20, No. 3 (1st Release): Contains markings for a silver F-105D, 60-464, of the 53rd TFS, 36th TFW, red, blue, and yellow fin flash.

Otaki Kit Number OT2-20, No. 3 (2nd Release): Contains markings for an F-105D, 62-4328, 12th TFS, 18th TFW, tail code ZA, in two-tone green and tan over gray scheme.

1/100th SCALE KITS

Tamiya Kit Number PA 1026: Contains markings for three aircraft, all camouflaged.
- F-105D, 59-739, 354th TFS, 355th TFW, tail code RM
- F-105D, 60-428, 469th TFS, 388th TFW, tail code JV
- F-105D, 62-248, 12th TFS, 18th TFW, tail code ZA, yellow band on tail.

1/72nd SCALE KITS

AMT Kit Number A656: Contains markings for two aircraft.
- F-105D, 58-1173, FH-173, bare metal scheme
- F-105D, 61-159, 333rd TFS, 355th TFW, tail code RK, camouflage scheme.

Note: The blue on this sheet used for the USAF, U.S. Air Force, tail number, and national insignia, is a medium blue rather than being the correct dark insignia blue.

Hasegawa Kit Number JS-014: Contains markings for three aircraft.
- F-105D, 61-156, FH-156, TAC badge on tail, sharkmouth on nose, overall silver
- F-105D, 62-4375, 12th TFS, 18th TFW, tail code ZA, camouflaged
- F-105D, 60-435, 12th TFS, 18th TFW, tail code ZA, camouflaged

Minicraft/Hasegawa Kit Number 014: Contains markings for three aircraft.
- F-105D, 61-132, 34th TFS, 388th TFW, tail code JJ, camouflaged, aircraft name "Hanoi Special," pilot Lt. David B. Waldrop III, 2 kill marks
- F-105D, 61-138, 563rd TFS, 23rd TFW, squadron insignia is included, camouflage
- F-105D, 59-1743, 34th TFS, 388th TFW, tail code JJ, camouflaged, aircraft name "Arkansas Traveler," pilot Col. Paul Douglas, 6 WW-II German kills, black, yellow, and green stripes on the main gear doors

Minicraft/Hasegawa Kit Number 1014: Contains Scale-Master decals for an F-105B, 57-5787, FH-787, 335th TFS, 4th TFW, green tail and nose bonds, chief's head insignia, bare metal scheme.

Minicraft Kit Number 122: Provides markings for an F-105B, 57-5814 in "Thunderbird" markings.

Monogram Kit Number 6808: Provides marking for an F-105D, 60-430, with a star-spangled tail band. However the kit is of a YF-105B.

Revell Kit Number H-231: Contains markings for an F-105D, 60-511, camouflage. The kit is of the prototype, not an F-105D.

1/72nd SCALE SHEETS

ESCI Sheet Number 87: Contains markings for four F-105Ds.
- F-105F, 63-8276, 419th TFTS (ex 4519th), 23rd TFW, tail code MG, pilot Lt. E. Taylor, aircraft name "The Beno Bitch/Angel," camouflage. Note: The Beno Bitch marking and the little man insignia are too small. They appear to be closer to 1/100th scale.
- F-105D, 61-169, FH-169, 563rd TFS, 23rd TFW, red and white rudder stripes, overall silver
- F-105D, 68-1743, 34th TFS, 388th TFW, tail code JJ, aircraft name "Arkansas Traveler," pilot Col. Paul Douglas, 6 WW-II German kills, black, yellow, and green stripes on the main gear doors.
- F-105D, 59-739, 354th TFS, 355th TFW, tail code RM, beer-drinking bulldog art.

Note: Additionally, this sheet has art for Foley's Folly/Ohio Express, which appears to be in 1/144th scale, the Iron Butterfly, Bonnie and Clyde art for F-105s, and an incorrect red "Hanoi Special." Also included is a chief's head, but this seems closer to 1/100th scale. No other markings for these aircraft are provided.

Microscale Sheet Number 72-95 (Camouflaged F-105s): Contains markings for five aircraft.
- F-105F, 63-176, 419th TFTS, (ex 4519th), 23rd TFW, tail code MG, aircraft name, "The Beno Bitch/Angel, pilot, Lt. E. Taylor
- F-105D, 59-771, 469th TFS, 388th TFW, tail code JV, aircraft name, Foley's Folly/Ohio Express, River Rats insignia, pilot, Captain Pete Foley
- F-105D, 62-346, 469th TFS, 388th TFW, tail code, JV, aircraft name "Good Golly Miss Molly," pilot, Col. Walker
- F-105D, 59-743, 34th TFS, 388th TFW, tail code JJ, aircraft name "Arkansas Traveler," pilot, Col. Douglas, 6 WW-II German kills
- F-105D, 61-132, 34th TFS, 388th TFW, tail code JJ, pilot, Lt. Waldrop, two kills

Note: A sharkmouth is given with no placement instructions. Further the stenciling given for these camouflaged aircraft is, for the most part, stenciling used on bare metal and silver doped aircraft, and is incorrect.

Microscale Sheet Number 72-96 (Silver F-105s): Contains markings for five F-105Ds.
- F-105D, 59-1719, FH-719, 355th TFS, 4th TFW, green nose and tail bands, chief's head insignia.
- F-105D, 62-4408, FH-408, 561st TFS, 23rd TFW, black and yellow tail checks, TAC insignia on tail.
- F-105D, 61-172, FH-172, 562nd TFS, 23rd TFW, sharkmouth, 3 olive drab fuselage bands
- F-105D, 61-100, FH-100, 49th TFW, red, yellow, and blue lightning bolt on nose, red, yellow, and blue "wing" on 49th TFW crest on tail.
- F-105D, 61-155, FH-155, 53rd TFS, 36th TFW, red, blue, and yellow diagonal tail stripes.

Microscale Sheet Number 72-144, (USAF MiG Killers): Provided markings for an F-105D, 60-504, 357th TFS, 355th TFW, tail code RU, aircraft name, "Memphis Belle II," camouflaged, light gray fin tip, yellow canopy rail with no name

Microscale Sheet Number 72-178, (Silver F-105s): Provides markings for three aircraft.
- F-105D, 61-144, FH-144, 4th TFW, green, yellow, blue, red nose and tail stripes
- F-105D, 61-169, FH-169, 563rd TFS, 23rd TFW, red and white rudder stripes, black spade on tail
- F-105D, 59-1766, FH-766, red bordered black and yellow checkered tail stripe

Microscale Sheet Number 72-179 (Camouflaged F-105s): Contains markings for six aircraft.
- F-105D, 60-514, 49th TFW
- F-105D, 59-822, 414th TFS, 355th TFW, tail code RE, aircraft name "The Polish Glider," Polish eagle on nose
- F-105G, 63-291, 17th WWS, tail code JB, aircraft name "Mutley," with sharkteeth
- F-105D, 0-10129, Sacramento AMA, red nose stripe, SAMA crest on fin and gear doors
- F-105G, 63-438, 66th FWS, 57th FWW, tail code WA
- F-105D, 59-739, 354 TFS, 355th TFW, tail code RM, bulldog art

Note: As with other Microscale sheets with camouflaged F-105s, Microscale has incorrectly provided stenciling for bare metal aircraft or those painted silver.

Microscale Sheet 72-304: Provides markings for an F-105B, 57-5776, of the New Jersey Air National Guard. The aircraft has bicentennial markings on the tail. Camouflaged scheme.

Note: Microscale incorrectly spelled "New Jersey" as "New Jersy," and again provided stenciling primarily for a silver F-105.

Modeldecal Sheet Number 10: Provides markings for an F-105D, 62-229, 357th TFS, 355th TFW, tail code RU, aircraft name "Jeanie II," pilot LTC Jack Spillers, "I Dream of Jeanie" and magic lamp art on fuselage.

1/48th SCALE KIT

Monogram Kit Number 5806: Provides markings for an F-105G, 63-291, 17th WWS, aircraft name "Mutley," tail code JB, with sharkteeth.

1/48th SCALE SHEETS

Fowler Sheet 4809 (Camouflaged F-105F/Gs): Provides markings for five aircraft.
- F-105F, 63-274, 4th TFS, 388th TFW, tail code JE, aircraft name, "Great Speckled Bird"
- F-105F, 63-8329, 4th TFS, 388th TFW, tail code JE, aircraft name "Protestor's Protector/My Diane," Capt. Frank/Capt. Wiest on left canopy rails, Sgt. Gimm/A1C Knaper on right canopy rails
- F-105G, 63-8305, 561st TFS, 23rd TFW, tail code MD
- F-105G, 63-8320, 561st TFS, 23rd TFW, tail code GA, yellow fin stripe, 3 MiG kills
- F-105G, 63-276, 35th TFW, tail code WW, TAC badges on tail, sharkteeth

Fowler Sheet 4810 (ANG/AFRes F-105F/Gs): Contains markings for four aircraft.
- F-105G, 63-274, Georgia ANG, sharkteeth, pilot Col. Jenkins, C/C Sgt. Jenkins, OUA ribbon, Maple leaf zap on fin, under wings -- "To Dobbins with love from the feminist fox and crew 80," yellow band with "Georgia" on tail
- F-105F, 63-365, 465th TFS, 607th TFG, AFRes, Tinker AFB, OK, blue tail band, Capt. Whipple on forward canopy rails, c/c TSgt. Hale, tail code SH
- F-105F, 63-309, 457th TFS, 301st TFW, AFRes, tail code TH, red fin stripe, Capt. Kirby on forward canopy rails, Doc Lansford on rear canopy rails
- F-105F, 44-13, 149th TFS, 192nd TFG, Virginia ANG, aircraft name "Flying Anvil," "Virginia" in white on tail, yellow band with black lightning bolt on tail

Fowler Sheet Number 4811 (Silver F-105Fs): Provides markings for three aircraft.
- F-105F, 63-274, 23rd TFW, blue intake trim
- F-105F, 63-8311, 49th TFW, wing badge with red, yellow and blue stripes on tail, yellow main gear doors
- F-105F, 63-8301, 36th TFW, yellow, red, and blue tail band, yellow wedges on forward fuselage

Note: All national insignia and major stenciling is provided.

If Fowler Decals are not available in your area, write to: Fowler Aviation, P.O. Box 148, Sunnymead, California 92388.

General Note: At press time for this book, the Monogram F-105G kit in 1/48th scale had not been released. Once *it is, we expect more decals to be released for it in 1/48th scale.*

REFERENCE LISTING

Note: Listed here are references on the F-105 that should prove helpful in providing information and photographs of a different nature and format than what is presented in this publication. With each listing is a brief description of what that reference covers. There are many fine references on the F-105, and they cannot all be listed here. The fact that a given reference is not listed is not intended to reflect unfavorably on that reference.

1. Archer, Robert D. The Republic F-105 "Thunderchief," Aero Publishers, Inc., Fallbrook, California, 1969.

An excellent book covering the development of the F-105 through the -F version. Unit histories, specifications, and other data is included.

2. Drendel, Lou, F-105 Thunderchief, in Action, Squadron Signal Publications, Carrollton, Texas, 1974.

Good publication with numerous photographs showing markings and some details. Contains coverage of the Thud in combat.

3. Van Geffen, Theodore W., Republic F-105 Thunderchief, Profile Publications, Berkshire, England, 1971.

A short concise book covering the Thunderchief's development and service. Contains charts and listings of data, operational data, and specifications.

4. Scutts, J.C., F-105 Thunderchief, Charles Scribner's Sons, New York, N.Y., 1981.

This book is the most accurate, up-to-date, and complete book available on the history of the F-105. Contains extensive coverage of the development and combat use of the Thunderchief.

5. F-105, Koku Fan Special Number 33, Bunrin-Do, Japan, 1973.

Excellent source for photographs showing the colors and markings of the F-105. Japanese text.

6. Mizaki, Joe, and Peter Maucus, "Thud, Goes the Weasel!," Airpower, Volume II, Number 1, January 1981, Page 24, Sentry Books, Inc.

Good article with emphasis on the use of the F-105 in Vietnam.

7. Jablonski, Ron, "Twilight for the USAF's Thud," Air Combat, Volume 6, Number 6, November 1981, Page 32, Challenge Publications.

Although it contains a few errors (J-57 instead of J75 engines, and drawings of an F-105F and F-105G with short tails), this article reviews the "Thuds" service with the U.S. Air Force.

8. Linn, Don, "F-105 Photo Essay," IPMS Quarterly, Volume 17, Number 3, Spring 1982, Page 5, IPMS/USA.

Excellent photographic coverage of the F-105 by Detail & Scale author Don Linn. Contains general and detail shots.

9. Kinzey, Bert, "Thunder Jockey," UPDATE, Volume 10, Number 5, IPMS/USA, Page 118.

Short article about Pete Foley, the third man to complete two tours and 200 missions in an F-105 over Vietnam. Contains drawings and explanations on how to update the Minicraft/Hasegawa F-105D, and shows Foley's markings in detail.